DESTINED TO
Succeed

DESTINED TO
Succeed

Unraveling and Upholding God's Purpose for Your Life

DR. ABDUL K. SESAY

Ordering Information:

For orders and inquiries, please contact:
1-888-375-9818
www.toplinkpublishing.com
bookorder@toplinkpublishing.com

Printed in the United States of America

CONTENTS

FOREWORD

The author of this book, "Destined to Succeed," Reverend Dr. Abdul K. Sesay, has been my Pastor for 14 years. As the Administrator of the Church founded by Pastor Sesay, the Kings and Priests Church International (KPCI) ministries, I have watched Pastor Abdul grow as an anointed man of God and helped teach and develop many of his followers to believe and spread the good news of the Kingdom of God. Pastor Sesay is not only a great preacher of the Word of God, but an inspiring teacher of life's lessons, a passionate and committed man of God who cares for people and desires to transform lives and win souls for Jesus Christ our Lord. It is from this perspective that Pastor Seasy decided to write "Destined to succeed". The inspiration for this book was derived from a sermon Pastor Seay preached to his congregation. It was such a firing sermon, laden with cogent examples from the Pastor's own personal life that gripped the congregation with outpouring emotions. We could see that even the Pastor was touched by his own preaching, and was totally transformed by his recollection of the painful moments in his life when the road to success seemed so rocky and efforts towards success seemed daunting or impossible. How the Pastor persevered and overcame those huddles, standing on the promise of the Word of God, is the central theme of "Destined to Succeed."

Practically this book teaches the labor and harvest of mankind, and how the reward of our labor is tied to the biblical concept of predestination. Christians believe that everything that happens to man in this world was predestined from conception. Pastor Abdul expands on the concept of predestination by teaching that since man was made in God's own image, and God is not a failure, then it is man's destiny to succeed if only man works in the ways of the Lord. I personally believe that Rev. Dr. Sesay fits the profile to write this book because of his background and his testimonies. He is himself a practical example of the focused Pastor who has followed and applied biblical rules and principles to achieve success. In this acclaimed book Pastor Sesay ventures to challenge believers to work hard, follow the principles espoused in the scriptures and put their faith in God and not in themselves. Pastor Sesay strongly believes that following these principles will no doubt lead to success that would enrich the lives of Christians.

Destined to Succeed opens our eyes to see that God is not an illusion conjured by an eloquent preacher, but the one Whom, if we believe in Him, and follow the principles as written in the Bible, we will surely succeed. Pastor Sesay epitomizes this hope and dream because he started his church from extremely humble beginnings. And today, Pastor Sesay and his followers broke ground and built their own church from foundation to completion right here in the heart of Montgomery County, Maryland, United States of America. This is a success that I believe came by way of predestination and working in the principles of God, if you follow the personal life of Pastor Sesay. In fact, according to popular opinion, Pastor Sesay is probably the only pastor here in

Maryland, from his native Sierra Leone, who has built his own church here in the state of Maryland in recent years. I mean the pastor who break ground, laid the foundation and build until completion, with the help of his congregation. That man of God is Pastor Sesay, and I am proud of what we all achieved together as a church. This is an extraordinary achievement by Pastor Sesay and may God continue to bless him.

The book speaks of "COURAGE: "It takes courage to operate in the realm of success. In most cases, the path to success may not be smooth. There are challenges that one may encounter on the pathway to success. Such challenges may lead to a detour if the service of courage is not deployed. Courage is the screw that helps to hold the component together during adverse conditions".

Rev. Dr. Sesay quoted: "Joshua 1:6-7 "Be strong and of good courage, for to this people you shall divide as an inheritance the land which I swore to their fathers to give them........"

Pastor Sesay said *"This statement and quotation from the bible has kept me strong in the weak days and given me hope when all is lost. I particularly like this quote because it tells us that "Destined to Succeed" does not mean we are not going to meet road blocks"*

Truly we have roadblocks in life but that is just a detour. *It means a lot to me to write this foreword because I see firsthand how Rev. Dr. Sesay strives towards success at all cost. Every day I work with him either in the office or when he is preaching, I hear him talk about success and how to attain it.*

Readers, I trust that *after reading this book, you will understand that failure is not your portion if you work in the ways of the Lord. . Rev. Dr.*

Sesay's own life story is indeed a pillar of strength. He came to America with a small suitcase and a vision to Gather God's People, to teach them the saving knowledge of Jesus Christ. And today, to God be the glory, he is the shepherd of a fourteen thousand square feet building that has both a sanctuary that seats 450 people and a fellowship hall and runs a Christian school. *This church is the place for worship for a multicultural congregation that is thirsty for more of the Word every Sunday. To say that Dr. Sesay is qualified to write a book on success is an understatement. As readers will discover for themselves, Pastor Sesay's own life story is a testimony to the fact that he is an authority on the subject of success.*

Doris Felicia Williams

PREFACE

*D*ESTINED TO SUCCEED is a guide to unveiling God's purpose for your life. The concept of discovering God's plan for your life is vital, as it will serve as a navigating tool to keep you on track towards your destiny. **When you discover your spiritual DNA, you will be amazed to know that success is not an option in God's agenda for you,** but it is your predestination. The first step towards discovering your predestination, however, is pursuing the purpose of God in your life, as that is paramount in achieving success. *Destined to Succeed* outlines strategies for discovering and pursuing God's plan for your life.

APPRECIATION

With a humble heart, I like to acknowledge Apostle Mama Dora Dumbuya for the foundation she laid in my life. As the scripture states, *"if the foundation be destroyed what can the righteous do?"* Mama laid a solid foundation in my life that can allow me to build and continue to add apartments to the building because the foundation is solid enough to accommodate the structure. This book *Destined to Succeed* is anchored on a solid foundation. I am grateful to Mama and the entire leadership of Jesus Is Lord Ministries Inc. Tower Hill, Freetown, for helping me to discover my God given potential. Beyond her spiritual discovery of my God given talent Mama erected and supported a solid foundation in my life and ministry. I am thankful that my foundation was not destroyed, all because I had Mama's guidance and support for our church that helped to align me with my destiny.

My heartfelt appreciations goes to my biological mother Madam Marie Conteh; thank you mother for your drastic effort of running away with me at the age of two in order to preserve my life. I am also using this medium to acknowledge my two beautiful daughters Absat Abigail Sesay and Anna Sesay for your support to the work of the ministry that the Lord has committed to my charge. Absat and Anna, I know it's not easy for you as pastor's children especially when you sometimes think that there are so many constraints as you cannot participate in some of the things your peers are doing. Both of you are actively supporting me in ministry and I am really grateful for both of you.

To all the pastors, ministers, leaders and members of Kings & Priests Court Int'l Ministries Inc. my appreciation goes to you all for believing in me and the vision *"Gather My People'* of this dynamic ministry. A big thank you to you all, I pray that you will unfold the secret of success through the reading of this book *–Destined to Succeed.*

Also my heartfelt appreciation goes to Ms. Doris Williams, Administrator of Kings & Priests Court Int'l Ministries, Egerton Johnson and Rev. Sarah Samura, for assisting in typing of the manuscript of this book. A special thanks to Princetta Jarry for designing the book cover. The cover photo is an original picture taking at Hobart, Australia by Pastor Abdul Karim Kamara.

And, last but not least, my thanks go to David Bobby Gboyor, writer, journalist, legal professional and friend of KPCI, for his review and insightful comments on the manuscript.

DEDICATION

I dedicate this book to some people to whom I am indebted for their input and contributions in my life. The old cliché that states "it takes a village to raise a child" is distinctively applicable in my life. I want to use this opportunity to recognize and appreciate all those who have been spiritual mothers and others in my life. Thank you for all your efforts.

Specifically, I dedicate the writings of this book to Madam Henrietta Yansaneh in England, Madam Marie Kpakima and Mr. Andrew Kpakima Senior, USA; the late Madam Isata Kamara commonly known as Atta, and Mrs. Hawa Turay of Sierra Leone. You all believed in me when I was nothing. You saw beyond my present situation at that time. You invested your time and resources in my life that helped in developing me to be the man that I am today. To God be the glory. God gives a vision to a person; however it is the people that read the vision that will run with it.

Habakkuk 2:2 "And the Lord answered me, and said, Write the vision, and make it plain upon tables, that he may run that readeth it." In order words the readers of your vision will be part of the implementers of the vision. You read my vision and you ran with it without any reservation. You were there for me from the beginning, your confidence in me is greatly appreciated and I am glorifying God on your behalf.

This book is dedicated to all those who have been deprived of success, orphans and less fortunate children around the world.

INTRODUCTION

Destined to Succeed was intended to be a sermon to the congregation of Kings and Priests Court International Ministries (KPCI), but the subject matter of the book, "success," turns out to be of such universal application to mankind that it touches the life of everyone. Man's fundamental purpose on this earth is to fulfill the will of God, and that is to believe in Him, obey His word, and live it by submitting to the dictates of His Commandments so that man may inherit the Kingdom of God. In addition to salvation as God's purpose for man's life on earth in the grand scheme of things, God also purposes that man was born to succeed not only in inheriting the Kingdom of God, but also to subdue and have dominium over the things of this earth because God made man in his own image (Genesis 1:26 "And God said, Let us make man in our image, after our likeness: and let them have dominion over the fish of the sea, and over the fowl of the air, and over the cattle, and over all the earth, and over every creeping thing that creepeth upon the earth."

Consequently, if God the Almighty, the Beginning and the End, the Alpha and the Omega, made man in His own image, then man was born to succeed because God is not a failure and his words never fail. In other words, success is God's predestination for man ordained from conception. From a biblical perspective success is equated to a birthright, but not the birthright you inherit from your father and mother, which comes on a silver platter. Success is the birthright man inherits from God in His own image, which comes at conception and therefore it is in our DNA. This success cannot be taken for granted for the simple reason that man had fallen from Grace by sin, and man must now be resurrected through His only begotten son, our Lord Jesus Christ. And because achieving salvation itself is a work in progress for mankind, success, in all its worldly manifestations, is a work in progress because it is a reward that comes from God to His Children who labor in righteousness. Success is therefore a blessing from God that is not founded on greed or avarice, but on the word of God. Although man is destined to succeed according to the word of God, real and enduring success is not success at all cost; it is not success at the expense of righteousness or faithfulness, but success as is ordained by God for every single one of His children.

Just as no two human beings may have the exact same DNA, so also is the fact that no two people are destined to have the same measure of success no matter how hard they work for it. Therefore brethren, let us honor and celebrate success in others more successful than we may be because God has predestined them for that level of success. Let ye not be judged for your success and do not ye judge others because they are more successful for only God can. It is God's plan for every man to be successful according to his works. 3 John 2- "Beloved, I wish above all things that thou mayest proper and be in health, even as thy soul prospereth." And therefore only He can judge man by what measure of success he hath and by what means he obtained success thereof."

My purpose for writing this book *Destined to Succeed* is to empower my brethren to believe that mankind is endowed with the power to succeed and that man must work on the path of righteousness towards success. And, I wish that by reading this book, brethren will behold and have understanding that success is not just about the things of this world, but that the greater measure of success is to inherit the Kingdom of God because the Bible says "what does it profit a man to inherit the whole world and loses the Kingdom of God. (Mark 8:36) "For what shall it profit a man, if he shall gain the whole world, and lose his own soul?" In *Destined to Succeed*, my goal is to explain success from a holistic point of view, a two-dimensional view of success as hard work towards man's own personal success on earth as preordained, and success in gaining eternal life in the Kingdom of God. I have sought to explain what success means and differentiated types of successes. I have also urged brethren to reject certain types of and means to success, or manner of success, and how to manage and sustain success once attained; but I do not judge any for achieving success because only God has the exclusive authority to do so. My prayer is that God will bless and reward your works and you shall be successful according to His Word.

Success is therefore a blessing from God that is not founded on greed or avarice

CHAPTER ONE

Success is your Predestination

God gave us the power to replenish the earth and subdue it. In the context of this book, I want you to understand God's original intention for you since the foundation of the world. God's designed purpose for you is that mankind will succeed because you are created to replicate God on earth. The scripture echoes the words of God *"Let us make man in our image and likeness and let them have dominion."* So originally man was created to dominate the earth. How can you have dominion in your possession and then becomes a failure? It was not God's plan for you to fail. It is his plan for you to succeed. Success has gain; there is glory in winning. The basic truth of success is for you to know that it is your birthright from God. You have to know it and conceive the truth that success is in your DNA. It is your predestination, and your birthright as a child of God, and you need to walk in that dimension. Brethren you need to begin to operate in that realm that you are predestined to succeed in life. You are not a failure. As a matter of fact, for you to fail is to fall short of God's purpose for your life. He did not design you to be a failure. The Bible says in Genesis 1:28 that even after God created man, He blessed them. He blessed them because he wants them to be a success.

* + + ◆ + + +

Genesis 1:28-29 "And God blessed them, and God said unto them, be fruitful, and multiply, and replenish the earth, and subdue it: and have dominion over the fish of the sea, and over the fowl of the air, and over every living thing that moveth upon the earth. And God said, Behold, I have given you every herb bearing seed, which is upon the face of all the earth, and every tree, in which is the fruit of a tree yielding seed; to you it shall be for meat."

+ + ◆ ◆ + + +

Mostly, we quote these scriptures when we think about procreation and this same scripture talks about success. It talks about having dominion and also *"replenish"* which means 'bring after you.' You are born to succeed. You will not be a failure in the name of Jesus. Knowing and operating in God's purpose for your life is a pathway to success.

Success has gain; there is glory in winning

What does it mean to be successful? Success can be defined as having a favorable outcome. On the other hand, success can be defined as having things turn out as planned. When things begin to work in the ways God planned it for you, then you are heading for a successful life. Success is also traced

As a matter of fact, for you to fail is to fall short of God's purpose for your life

to attaining a goal or to attain the desired result. I believe that success is the continuous attainment of God's set goals in your life. One has to be ready to confront his or her failure. Confront your past and look up to Jesus Christ who is the author and finisher of your faith. Look at it this way; you have to confront failure because you cannot fail anymore. For you to fail is an abomination. Failure will rob you of your self-esteem. It will rob you of your prestige. It will rob you of God's glory. Failure will take away courage and boldness from you. You have to take a step and know that God created you on this earth to succeed. Though Adam and Eve failed God, you are born to succeed. You can thrive on the foundation laid by Jesus Christ. You cannot be a failure anymore because you know your destiny. The Bible states in the book of Deuteronomy that God's plan is to make you the head and not the tail. You are designed to be above only and not beneath.

———————— •✦•✦•✦•✦•✦•✦• ————————

Deuteronomy 28:13 "And the Lord shall make thee the head, and not the tail; and thou shalt be above only, and thou shalt not be beneath; if that thou hearken unto the commandments of the Lord thy God, which I command thee this day, to observe and to do them."

———————— •✦•✦•✦•✦•✦•✦• ————————

It is clear that when you fail at something, there are places that you are supposed to show up you cannot show up because failure has taken what is supposed to be in you. You need to know that God designed you to be successful. A man that is successful cannot be beneath. It says that you are meant to be the "head

> **Success is also traced to attaining a goal or to attain the desired result.**

and not the tail." What differentiate the head and the tail? The head is up and the tail is behind. You will mostly see the head before you see the tail and God made you to be the head because you are born to succeed. It is not a coincident that God says in *Jeremiah 29:11 "I know the*

Confront your past and look up to Jesus Christ

plans I have for you, plans to prosper you and not to harm you, plans to give you hope and a future". So originally, God planned for you to be successful. He has designed it and nobody can change it. It is up to you to walk in that dimension, to believe that God designed you to be a success. Success is not by accident. It is a gift from God and a choice whether or not to accept it. My aspiration is for you to open your eyes and your understanding then it is up to you to make the choice. In the Old

You can thrive on the foundation laid by Jesus Christ.

Testament you will understand how Moses was encouraging the people to choose life over death.

Deuteronomy 30:15-16 "See, I have set before thee this day life and good, and death and evil;In that I command thee this day to love the Lord thy God, to walk in his ways, and to keep his commandments and his statutes and his judgments, that thou mayest live and multiply: and the Lord thy God shall bless thee in the land whither thou goest to possess it."

It is a matter of choice. I don't know who want to fail or like to fail. Everybody wants to be successful so it is a choice that you have to make.

Make the right choice to succeed in life. Set your priorities right. Be assured success is God's original design for you. When success is gained outside God's purpose and will, it does not last. You need to attain success that will speak of God's sovereignty. It must reflect God's glory, and

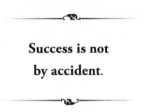

Success is not by accident.

people must recognize it in you. There are three types of success that I will want us to focus on in this book.

Human Success

Human success is success that is based on human principles and methodologies. This type of success is based on tradition and sensual attributions. Yes, God has given unto us wisdom, knowledge and understanding on how we can help ourselves. The dilemma beyond human success is a success that does not recognize God as the source of providence. The human success does not give room to others. It is characterize by selfish ambition. This is the reason why people crave success and discourage others from getting it. Some human successes are developed by the use of charms while others are attained by ambitious principles like sorcery. Human success has no regard for Christian values and such type of success is characterized by troubles and struggles. Some human successes are done through satanic covenant and because of this there is a payback that one has to give. This is why you see some people making a yearly sacrifice. Like I said earlier, human success does not create room for God. The Bible tells us in the book of Genesis about human beings who were succeeding in building what was called the *"Tower of Babel"*. Clearly by their wisdom, they were succeeding in building the tower. Their determination was to build the tower to reach up to the heavens. The fact suggests that because human success is based on sensual ideology, they had no Christian values or respect credited to God for their endeavor. They said to themselves, "We build this tower that we may make name for ourselves."

Genesis 11:4-5 "And they said, Go to, let us build us a city and a tower, whose top may reach unto heaven; and let us make us a name, lest we be scattered abroad upon the face of the whole earth. And the Lord came down to see the city and the tower, which the children of men build."

What is this scripture talking about? Selfishness! It was all about them and God in his wisdom put a stop to it. This was how it ended. He confused them. He divided their tongues so that they could not speak in one language anymore. You should strive not to settle just for human success and edge God out of your achievement or accomplishment. In addition human success is trying to succeed by utilizing illegal means and avenues. I normally state that if one cannot be proud of their achievement then it is yet to be done.

The dilemma beyond human success is a success that does not recognize God as the source of providence.

Satanic Success

This type of success is based on evil principles, principles contrary to God's word. Do you know that such principles always end in disgrace? When you read Esther Chapter Six, it talks about how Haman wanted to succeed through satanic manipulation. At the end of the day, he ended up in disgrace. He was plotting against Mordecai, a servant of God. Haman plotted to kill Mordecai and the Jews in a bid to attain success. Sometimes success through evil is a so-called success, but it is transient and will not last. We can see that in the world in which we are living, people want to succeed at the expense of others. When some people want to succeed, they take the names of other people to sorcerers to exploit them of their blessing, their success and prosperity. The bible says cause does not act causeless. Even in man-made law, there is something called equity. The fundamental principle of equity is fairness and justice, and so those who come to equity must come with clean hands. .

Satanic success works with satanic people. The bible says we wrestle not against flesh and blood but against principalities and powers in high places. Therefore think good and the devil will flee, think evil and the devil will use it for and against you. Some are carrying charms and satanic objects in their wallets and their bags all around because they have to follow the instructions given to them for success; some folks have to put concoction on their bodies before they walk out of their homes, simply for them to gain favor or fame. Such individuals discredit the ingredients in body creams or lotions and vaseline. They think it does not work for them but concoction is what works for them. They have to apply it in a bid to attain success. That does not produce result. It is a satanic success. Everything that Satan gives, Satan will always demand a payback because Satan will request for something else in return.

1Thessalonians 5:22 "Abstain from all appearance of evil."

In Genesis chapter four Cain wanted to succeed at the expense of his brother Abel. He saw the favor over the life of his brother and he wanted to be in that position. What did he do? He killed Abel.

Genesis 4:8-9 "And Cain talked with Abel his brother: and it came to pass, when they were in the field, that Cain rose up against Abel his brother, and slew him. And the Lord said unto Cain, Where is Abel thy brother? And he said, I know not: Am I my brother's keeper?

It is sadden to know that people are killing others in a bid to succeed. Some will say, "man die, before man live". In that regard they will try to kill someone to pave their own way for success. Such a success is not permanent; it will fade away at some point in time.

1Thessalonians 5:15 See that none render evil for evil unto any man; but ever follow that which is good, both among yourselves, and to all men."

Success gained by satanic means has a lot of strings attached to it. The recipient of such success will have to suffer the consequences of the devil at the end.

Proverbs 13:11 "Wealth gotten by vanity shall be diminished: but he that gathereth by labor shall increase."

Covenant or Divine Success

Covenant or divine success is a success that is based on God's Word and principles. This type of success is motivated by God's will. This type of success can be delayed but it is sure and certain. The Bible says in ***Psalm 1:1-3 "Blessed is the man that walketh not in the counsel of the ungodly, nor standeth in the way of sinners, nor sitteth in the seat of the scornful. But his delight is in the law of the LORD; and in his law doth he meditate day and night. And he shall be like a tree planted by the rivers of water that bringeth forth his fruit in his season; his leaf also shall not wither; and whatsoever he doeth shall prosper"***.

In a covenant or divine success, man does not walk in the counsel of the ungodly in order to attain success. Rather man will need to follow the principles of God, follow the mandate of God, follow the directions of God, and follow the

> **Covenant or divine success is a success that is based on God's Word and principles**.

prerogatives of God in a bid to attain success. Precisely the Bible puts it this way, he shall be like a tree that will never lack moisture, will never lack nutrients, will never lack supply, and that is what God designed you to be. You will succeed. You must operate in that dimension. Know that it is your predestination to succeed. God prepares and plan it for you to succeed. God made it to happen in order for you not to be a failure. It may be slow, but it is sure. Wait patiently for divine success because after it begins, you will never dwindle. As long as you stay within the principles of God, it will not regress, trials may come but your success will always progress.

Success is God's will and plan for you. Success is measured by who you are in Christ. People sometimes tend to misunderstand success. When they look at people who are successful, they say he/she has a good car.

Know that it is your predestination to succeed.

But success is beyond the good car. You are limiting what God designed for you. Your success is beyond a car and house because when it comes from God, it keeps flowing. Your success begins when you realize that you are born with a purpose and determine to seek out that purpose. God wants you to have dominion. He wants you to succeed. When you have dominion, every other thing is subjective to you.

Acts 22:10 "And I said, what shall I do, LORD? And the Lord said to me, Arise, and go into Damascus; and there it shall be told you of all things which are appointed for you to do".

This is talking about Saul who later became Paul when he was persecuting the church of God. On his way to Damascus, he got struck by lightning. The Bible says he was confused, he was in a state of despair and he did not know what to do.

Your success begins when you realize that you are born with a purpose

The voice of the Lord ministered unto him and told him to go to a certain place where he could wash his eyes. In light of Paul's discovery, it is therefore necessary for you to understand that success in life begins with discovering your purpose. **c**

Jeremiah 29:11 "For I know the thoughts that I think toward you, saith the Lord, thoughts of peace, and not of evil, to give you an expected end."

What is your purpose? Why are you here on earth? Why did God create you and place you on this planet? Why did God say I have a purpose for you? Success is not by mistake. It is your predestination. In the words of the Scriptures, Paul said that it pleases the Lord who separated me from my mother's womb.

Galatians 1:15 "But when it pleased God, who separated me from my mother's womb, and called me by his grace."

You may be born out of wedlock or born in poverty but God has a purpose for you in life to succeed. It is not where you were born, or to whom you were born to but it is a question of understanding God's purpose for your life. He set you apart and separated you while you were in your mother's womb. He sees you and knows what he destined you to be, your future shines so bright it burns. You are born to succeed. The ball is in your court. If you want to sit on it, sit on it. If you want to act on it, then act on it because you cannot be a failure.

I can write, preach and testify of this very truth because my life is a living testimony. The day I discovered God's purpose for my life, that was the day I terminated every thought of failure in my mind. My perception changed completely. Before I received salvation I was constantly affected by inferiority complex due to my family background. Brethren God's plan for my life became clear, magnified, bold and certain when I made a concerted effort to follow his principles. I regained my consciousness of God's purpose for my life and realized that I was born with a mission. Folks, pursue, seek and fight for success.

Sometimes, people think that success is tied to a particular region. For example, I may not belong to the royal family of England but the Bible tells me that I belong to a royal priesthood destined for greatness. You are a king or queen on your own. God gave you a domain, a terrain to rule and manifest the greatness of God.

1Peter 2:9 "But ye are a chosen generation, a royal priesthood, an holy nation, a peculiar people; that ye should shew forth the praises of him who hath called you out of darkness into his marvelous light."

When you think that success belongs to a particular region, you will be distracted and that will cause you pain. It does not matter where you were born. Your beginning has nothing to do with your success. It is just there to complete the story. No wonder the Bible says *"Better of is the*

Folks, pursue, seek and fight for success.

end of things than the beginning thereof" (Ecclesiastes 7:8). It is not the starting, but the end. You are born to succeed and you will succeed.

Success is not a native of any particular place. It is for everyone. For example, we have people who are born and raised up in America but because they failed to discover the purpose of their lives, they are living in abject poverty. America is a nation full of opportunities for determined people yet people still live in depravity and failures.

Success is not by the complexion of your skin. To base success on complexion is the wrong concept; it is basically a recipe for failure. Shining right is not the same as shinning bright, according to Bishop David Oyedepo. Understanding God's purpose for your life is one of the first requirements for success. Some people have wrong concepts of success that is detrimental to exercising success as predestined by their creator. Success is a function of what you know from the word of God. When you apply it, you will begin to see success unfold. You will begin to see things come alive. The churches today need revelation in order to revolutionize our minds. Our minds have been negative for too long. Break out of the norm of failure and step into the realm of success.

> **Success is not a native of any particular place. It is for everyone.**

Until now, people regard Christians or pastors and church leaders as people of less value or dropouts. Some folks misunderstand the concept of success for believers. To substantiate their points, they quote examples in the bible to confuse people. They will compare the

> **Success is a function of what you know from the word of God.**

difficulty of a camel going through the eyes of a needle with a Christian becoming rich. This is a wrong concept because the Bible itself said, "money is a defense".

- - - - - - ✦ ✦ ✦ ✦ ✦ - - - - - -

Ecclesiastes 7:12 "For wisdom is a defense, and money is a defense: but the excellency of knowledge is, that wisdom giveth life to them that have it."

- - - - - - ✦ ✦ ✦ ✦ ✦ - - - - - -

As a Christian, you have to realize that you are created in God's image and blessed by God from birth. God said to you on the first day of your appearance on earth, *"be fruitful"*. Your perception needs to change and one needs to believe that he or she is designed for success. The devil takes advantage over us by ignorance but we will take advantage over him by our knowledge. Once you gain the knowledge that you are born to succeed, nothing will hold you back from being successful. The devil always tries to disrupt our intellect. Now that you have the knowledge, confront your failure. Apply biblical principles into your life and you will see them begin to unfold. The successes of believers are centered on God. With God in your life, success is guaranteed.

Apply biblical principles into your life and you will see them begin to unfold.

CHAPTER TWO

Allergic to Failure

In the previous chapter, I talked about three types of success, which are: Human Success, Satanic Success, and Covenant or Divine Success. According to the Bible success is designed for the saints of God. In *3rd John 1:2, the Bible says "Beloved, I wish above all things that thou mayest prosper and be in health, even as thy soul prospereth"*. As a saint, you have the qualifications to succeed in life because God is calling you His beloved. The journey of every believer should end up in success. You are born to be the head and not the tail. This is an indication that you are a star. There is a universal crave for success. Everyone wants to succeed. Some may speak about success, some may want to try it and some may even oppose it because they do not have it. As a child of God, you are a candidate for success. You were born to succeed and to fail is abnormal. Failure will cause you to look inferior but when you begin to succeed in life, it guarantees peace and brings people around you. Remember success attracts and failure repels. Some people think that success is not for believers. That is the wrong conception about success.

Deuteronomy 28:13 "And the Lord shall make thee the head, and not the tail; and thou shalt be above only, and thou shalt not be beneath."

The wrong concept about success is the misconception that it is impossible to be successful and be holy as well. Folks, you can still be righteous and be successful. It is a notion that requires change; we have been rejuvenated and transformed by the blood of Jesus Christ, and we must strive to change the pattern. The word "transformation" is a combination of two words: "trans" and "formation". Trans

You were born to succeed and to fail is abnormal.

means change and formation means patterns. So once you are transformed, the pattern has changed. In the past, people look at churchgoers as people who are broke, deprived, disappointed and frustrated. But now that you know what you know in the word, nobody can look down upon you and you accept those conditions. Take a snap at my transformation, sleeping on the benches in the church back then in Freetown, to my present movement of being a global preacher. Only God can do such, the blessings are marvelous.

It is God's will for one to be successful. In this chapter, we are going to prove that success is from God. There is a wise saying that "success consists of a series of little daily efforts". Every little effort one puts to progress in a day will lead to success. In other words, success demands human efforts. In order to be successful in life, you must anchor your life in practicing biblical principles. Some unbelievers are successful not by dubious acts but because they discovered the principles of success outlined in God's word. If an unbeliever can succeed, why not you a covenanted child of God who understands the principles and knows that it is your right. It is your position to succeed. Let me reference my spiritual mother Apostle Mama Dora Dumbuya, a virtuous woman born in a small village in Bombali District called Kamatonkap in the Sella Limba Chiefdom. She accepted the call of God in 1983, started very small but today she is the leading pastor/preacher in Sierra Leone. She is one of the major reverends to host a crusade at the national stadium with an overwhelming crowd of people. From the village to a recipient of the honor of the Order of the Rokel award from the President of the Republic of Sierra Leone, an honor that is bestowed on distinguished individuals by the President

Every little effort one puts to progress in a day will lead to success.

of the nation. Check out her book "Cry Baby." The reason why we are not succeeding is because of lack of knowledge. The devil robs you of success because of lack of knowledge. But you are coming out of ignorance and stepping into success because the devil cannot rob you no more. We have people who do not believe that they are going to succeed in life because the devil has interfered with their brains. For instance, the evil voice of the devil makes people believe that there is no success in their family line; they look at it, they assess it, yes it is true, they confirm, my family is poor. But then tell yourself that does not mean that I should be poor regardless of my family misfortune. The devil engraved that concept of poverty in the mind of Gideon. Gideon grew up with the mindset of believing that nothing can liberate him and his family from the grip of poverty. Even when he had a theophanic encounter, reaffirming that God wants to make use of him to bring the best out of him, he was still in denial because of his failure mindset.

Judges 6:15 "And he said unto him, Oh my Lord, wherewith shall I save Israel? Behold, my family is poor in Manasseh, and I am the least in my father's house."

My Christian friends, success is not a tradition. It does not matter whom you were born to. The devil tried to lock your thoughts into thinking negative and this is because you lack knowledge. The devil can no longer cage you in failure because you have understood the principles of success, which is understanding God's purpose and desire for you and digging into the scriptures and discover the plans of God for humanity.

The bible says that when Jesus was born, he was wrapped in swaddling clothes and placed in a manger. They put him in an inn because there was no room. Where you were born may just contribute to your resume but does not determine who you are and what you are going to become. My belief is that Jesus never failed; therefore I will not fail in life. The Bible tells us in Job 1:3 "that when Job became successful, people began to itemize the substance and success of Job; what he *acquired,* what he *attained*, and what he *achieved* under God.

> **The devil can no longer cage you in failure**

Job 1:3 "Also, his possessions were seven thousand sheep, three thousand camels, five hundred yoke of oxen, five hundred female donkeys, and a very large household, so that this man was the greatest of all the people of the East."

If you read verse one of the same chapter, it says that Job was a man that pleased God. Job was a man that lived right and because of that he succeeded. He was a man who discovered his purpose in life. People who do not have a purpose are out of focus. The Bible says that Job understood his purpose and God blessed him.

Job 1:1 "There was a man in the land of Uz, whose name was Job; and that man was blameless and upright, and one who feared God and shunned evil."

Success speaks volume. However there are people that always try to bring the glory of God half way short. Think of the Nimrod generation that were aspiring to build a tower called the tower of Babel, their determination was to make name for themselves and not merely to give glory to God. This story is recorded in the book of Genesis chapter eleven. There is a story about a man who always provokes the glory of God. This man was carrying a briefcase with a sticker on it "Try my Jesus". When one reads this sticker, the next focus is on the man carrying the brief case. This is because people learn by example, the human mind moves in upward direction most of the time when measuring success. However, in the case of this man, when the eye moves from the briefcase to him, it does not add up. The man was not groomed well to match the Jesus that people would want to try. Even though we may be going through pain or struggle, the Bible says don't be like the Pharisees. Clean up and be presentable. I regard him as provoking Jesus because of his unkempt appearance for evangelism. My Jesus is not as poor as this man. Even when he became poor as an example for us, I believe that his clothes looked clean and smelled good. "He becameth poor that through his poverty you might become rich."

The things the man wore had worn out and even the shoe was saying "I lift up mine eyes unto the hills. Only God knows that I am a shoe because several nails have

Success speaks volume.

driven through me". So the shoe was crying. I am not saying that we should be curious about other people, but sometimes-positive curiosity is essential. This other man approached the man with the brief case and said to him 'if I try your Jesus, I will be worse'. Thank God for the discovery of God's purpose for our lives. Success is from God. When a successful person appears in our society, the whole community will survive because of him. That is why I encourage believers to encourage the rich and famous in the house of God; sometimes we discourage them from coming because we are intimidated by their show of riches. We start making comments on the cars they drive, the mansion they live in. Instead of focusing on what the rich people have let us focus on what they can do in the kingdom. Focus on how they can help with scholarship; improve the lives of the young ones. Success is not hidden no matter how hard you try to hide it.

Success that is not divine is selfish, because it does not want other people to succeed. The one that is of God is the one that helps others and show them the principles to succeed. There are varieties of successful characters in the book of Genesis. I want us to take a snapshot of one outstanding character- Joseph. He was successful up to the point that the house of an unbeliever became successful because of him. Potiphar's household enjoyed God's blessings because of Joseph.

Genesis 39:2-3 "And the Lord was with Joseph, and he was a prosperous man; and he was in the house of his master the Egyptian. And his master saw that the Lord was with him, and that the Lord made all that he did to prosper in his hand."

There may be trials or temptations on your path to success, but the end will justify the cause. The brothers of Joseph also hated Joseph who was a potential candidate for success. His brothers hated

Success is not hidden no matter how hard you try to hide it.

him to a point where they dropped him into a pit. Joseph knew that God created him to succeed. So despite the trials or opposition, Joseph proceeded to fulfill his potential. Abraham Lincoln who happens to be one of the greatest presidents of the United States once said, *"Success is the ability to go from failure to failure without losing your focus for your goal."* Peradventure, if Joseph had lost his focus when his brothers threw him into the pit he would not have been identified or recognized in the Book of Genesis as a successful man. In your bid to succeed in life, you will go through crucibles, you may face challenges but do not lose your focus. Joseph was sent into a pit and from the pit into Potiphar's house, from Potiphar's house into prison, and from the prison into the palace. Out of the four "P's" that happened in his life, the three were tragedies and the final "P" was the time of recognition.

The First was the PIT

Genesis 37:28 "Then there passed by Midianites merchantmen; and they drew and lifted up Joseph out of the pit, and sold Joseph to the Ishmeelites for twenty pieces of silver: and they brought Joseph into Egypt."

The Second was Potiphar's House

Genesis 39:1 "And Joseph was brought down to Egypt; and Potiphar, an officer of Pharaoh, captain of the guard, an Egyptian, bought him of the hands of the Ishmeelites, which had brought him down thither.

The Third was the Prison

Genesis 39:20 "And Joseph's master took him, and put him into the prison, a place where the king's prisoners were bound: and he was there in the prison."

The Fourth is the Palace: This Final "P" Erased all the Previous Ones

---

Genesis 41:39-41 "And Pharaoh said unto Joseph, Forasmuch as God hath shewed thee all this, there is none so discreet and wise as thou art: Thou shalt be over my house, and according unto thy word shall all my people be ruled: only in the throne will I be greater than thou. And Pharaoh said unto Joseph, See, I have set thee over all the land of Egypt."

When you go through challenges, you may face all these things but remember that there is a palace for you, because you are born to succeed. God has a purpose for you. Joseph proved to be a focal point for success. Despite all the challenges that he faced, he was allergic to failure. For you to fail is ungodly. Do not lose your focus. Keep striving because you are getting there. Success is not anti-godliness.

Things to Prove That Success is from God.

Every Good Gift is from God:

Firstly the Bible says in *James 1:17 that "Every good gift and every perfect gift is from above, and cometh down from the Father of lights, with whom is no variableness, neither shadow of turning"*. Therefore, success is a gift from God. Success is an attribute of divinity because God said let me create man and let him have dominion.

No Father Wants his Child to Fail:

Secondly, if you are a child of God you should know that you are created for success because no man wants his child to fail. No matter how bad your child is you still want that child to succeed. If I may ask you a question, that is: is it true or false? Yes, that puts you in the position of success.

Success is an attribute of divinity

Genesis 25:5-6 "And Abraham gave all that he had to Isaac. But Abraham gave gifts to the sons of the concubines which Abraham had; and while he was still living he sent them eastward, away from Isaac his son, to the country of the east." God does not want you to fail. As a child of God, he does not want you to fail. To fail is to disappoint God.

Father's Pride:

Thirdly, God is proud of your success. Some people do not even have confidence that God is proud of them. God is proud of your achievements. He is proud when you fulfill your goals. For example, when a child performs well in a sport activity when his/her parents are in the audience, everyone around them can tell that they are the parents because they will cheer their child along the way and give a standing ovation when appropriate. They will say, "That's my son" or "That's my daughter." Imagine God standing on the stands applauding you because of your success. Do not allow anyone to infuse you with the concept that success is not from God. The word of God states that he finds pleasure in our success because his name is at stake.

———— ✦ ✦ ◆ ✦ ✦ ————

Psalms 149:4 "For the Lord takes pleasure in His people;
He will beautify the humble with salvation."

———— ✦ ✦ ◆ ✦ ✦ ————

Put a smile on God's face today because you have discovered your purpose.

A Father is Protective of his Child:

Fourthly, when God gives success, he protects it. He will build a hedge around it. The word of God says in the book of Ecclesiastes that God put fence around the success of His servants. It is stated in the scriptures that God will build a hedge around you and whosoever tries to go through it, the serpent will bite.

Imagine God standing on the stands applauding you because of your success.

———— ✦ ✦ ◆ ✦ ✦ ————

Job 1:10 "Have you not made a hedge around him,
around his household, and around all that he has on
every side? You have blessed the work of his hands, and
his possessions have increased in the land."

———— ✦ ✦ ◆ ✦ ✦ ————

Moreover, you are made of success that is immune to failure. You are born to succeed and you are allergic to failure. Success is not a barrier to heaven. The Bible specifies that Abraham was rich and he made it to heaven. Success is a matter of choice. We all know the story about "Lazarus and the rich man". Despite the fact that the man was rich, he died and went to hell; Lazarus on the other hand was poor but made it to heaven.

Parents are Supportive of their Children:

Finally, the Bible says that Jesus fought against failure. In the Book of Luke it appeared as if defeat had hit the brains and minds of Simon Peter and his crew. Peter was at the verge of giving up when support came for him from the Lord. Peter had used all his ideologies on how to catch fish throughout the night, but he was unable to catch a single fish. The involvement of Jesus changed the equation. Peter yielded to the words of Jesus and said "Nevertheless, at thy word I will let down the net". When he let down the net, he was able to catch many fishes.

Luke 5:4-6 "When He had stopped speaking, He said to Simon, "Launch out into the deep and let down your nets for a catch."

But Simon answered and said to Him, "Master, we have toiled all night and caught nothing; nevertheless at your word I will let down the net." And when they had done this, they caught a great number of fish, and their net was breaking."

You are wired with the potential to succeed from birth. God wired mankind with a supportive system to follow. If mankind utilizes the principles in the supportive system created by God, there is huge possibility for success. It is my prayer before you complete the reading of this chapter in this book, that The Lord will give you direction for recovery of lost opportunities.

—— ✦✦✦✦✦ ——

Ephesians 2:10" For we are his workmanship, created in Christ Jesus for good works, which God prepared beforehand, that we should walk in them.

—— ✦✦✦✦✦ ——

You are born to succeed. The devil robbed you many times and still is because you were ignorant. Now that you have discovered God's purpose for your life, you are on your way out to success. He said in his word that he wish above all things that you may prosper. You are an exemption to failure. The secret to success is being revealed and exposed to you, act on it and see the reward.

> **You are wired with the potential to succeed from birth**.

—— ✦✦✦✦✦ ——

Deuteronomy 29:29 "The secret things belong unto the Lord our God: but those things which are revealed belong unto us and to our children forever, that we may do all the words of this law."

—— ✦✦✦✦✦ ——

Failing is part of the prerequisite for success. When you fail, it does not mean you are a failure. John Maxwell, the author of the book titled *Developing the Leader within You* says that "the enemy of best is good". As a matter of fact the scripture states that "one can fall seven times and rise again." I preached a message titled "Though I Fail, I am not a Failure." You are only a failure when you refuse to rise from the failed point or failed situation. When you fail or fall, try to get up, and if possible strive to wipe your image from the spot of fall and move to the next position.

Micah 7:8 "Do not rejoice over me, my enemy; when I fall, I will arise; When I sit in darkness, the Lord will be a light to me."

Evidently there is always light beyond the tunnel. Strive to overcome failure at any given time; failure is a robber. Reflecting back on my journey in ministry, I encountered several challenges and temptations that would have led me to give up in ministry but I refused to accept the gunshots of failure. For instance when our ministry was in search for a place to worship, we made several attempts to acquire or lease a property. We failed on

Failing is part of the prerequisite for success.

several occasions, and on some occasions we even lost funds. It was very painful knowing where our financial status was. However we refused to accept failures. Instead we constantly strived for a place that we can call home, and God made it possible for us. The Lord blessed us with a property right at the center of Montgomery County, Maryland. Many have asked me how I discovered the property. You can always overcome

Now that you have discovered God's purpose for your life, you are on your way out to success.

failure as long as you refuse to be a failure. There is abundant evidence to prove that most people who fear failure end up failing. The greatest risk is not taking a risk.

Reading through the quotes of one of America famous presidents on goodreads. com, Abraham Lincoln, who states that, "I am not concerned that you have fallen. I am concerned that you arise." It's my prayer

God is able to exceed your expectations.

that this book will inspire and challenge you to rise from every failed situation and take a fresh path to fulfilling your goal. Remember that nothing is too hard for the Lord to do.

Jeremiah 32:27 "Behold, I am the Lord, the God of all flesh: is there anything too hard for me?"

God is able to exceed your expectations. In this current era we must excel beyond boundaries. Technologically we are equipped in this generation than our forefathers, let us make use of the season and make an impact in God's name.

CHAPTER THREE

Operating in the Realm of Success

It is your predestination to succeed in life. You are a success. God designed you to be a success. In Chapter one, we looked at success being your predestination because God created you in His image and likeness. I highlighted the different types of success: Human, Satanic, and Covenant or Divine success. In Chapter two, I discussed how success is from God and how you can be allergic to failure because there is a success potential in you. In this chapter, I will talk on how you can operate in the dimension of success. You are meant to be creative regardless. We are a creative being. God says you are meant to be the head and not the tail but you have to contend for it. You have to activate it to make it happen. You cannot just lay back and say I am successful. You must maximize your potential for it to produce fruits. In as much as that success is God's desire for you, success is not cheap, it entails hard work.

There are people who think that success is for selected few. But I tell you; in the agenda of God you are qualified. The death of Christ has given you access into the presence of God at all times. How can you operate in that dimension? It entails the law of discovery. You have to explore to discover. When you discover, you make choices that guarantee success. When you discover what God has placed inside of you, it is this discovery that commands recovery. Every human being is choice bound. When you discover your

> **You must maximize your potential for it to produce fruits**.

potential, it will set you up on the foundation to excel in life. According to Bishop Oyedepo, "you need education for your foundation but you need your gifting for your destiny." When you discover the gift of God in you, it will provoke and activate you to succeed in life.

Proverbs 18:15-16 "The heart of the prudent getteth knowledge; and the ear of the wise seeketh knowledge. A man's gift maketh room for him, and bringeth him before great men."

It is your gifts that open rooms for greatness and brings recognition for you in the society and community that you live in. When the gift inside of you begins to show, then success will begin to unfold. In the kingdom of God no one is exempted from a gift, everyone is equipped with talents that need to be maximized. As long as you believe that God is the one sharing, just stand in line and you will receive your own fair share. You are a saint designed by God to excel in life. When you allow your talents to show up, it creates opportunities. Therefore, success entails engaging in the process of discovery. You begin to discover what your ambitions are and create a checklist for yourself. Assess yourself and see what motivates and activate it. Ask yourself "what ambitions do I have in life?" Do some check-ups on yourself. Know where you are going before you start your journey.

Courage:

It takes courage to operate in the realm of success. In most cases, the path to success may not be smooth. There are challenges that one may encounter on the pathway to success. Such challenges may lead to a detour if the service of courage is deployed. Courage is the screw that helps to hold the component together during an adverse condition.

God is the one sharing, just stand in line and you will receive your own fair share.

Joshua 1:6-7 "Be strong and of good courage, for to this people you shall divide as an inheritance the land which I swore to their fathers to give them. Only be strong and very courageous, that you may observe to do according to all the law which Moses My servant commanded you; do not turn from it to the right hand or to the left, that you may prosper wherever you go.

The task handed over to Joshua after the death of Moses was a great task. It will take bundles of courage for Joshua to lead the rest of the Israelites to reach the land promised to them. The Lord

It takes courage to operate in the realm of success.

encourages Joshua to be courageous. Courage to conquer and confront the oppositions; for Joshua, courage was something that he would need in facing his enemies and strength was what he needed to motivate his friends. Courage is the ability to control and calm fear in case of adversity as well as empowering individuals to be brave or bold in adverse circumstances.

It's on that premise that I conclude that in operating in the realm of success, courage is one of the prerequisites. Courage and strength are two brothers that virtually complement each other in the school of success.

* * * * * *

Ephesians 6:10 "Finally, my brethren, be strong in the Lord, and in the power of his might."

* * * * * *

Sailing on the sea of courage has been one of the anchors for my drive in my ministry. I refused circumstances and challenges to drag me down to the mud. Few years ago our ministry KPCI ran into a road block that took a lot from the

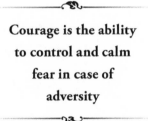

Courage is the ability to control and calm fear in case of adversity

church. The church decided to lease a property for its regular worship services and office activities with the notion that it will meet the zoning regulations in Prince Georges County. After the church invested almost the entire savings the church had at that time to rehabilitate and renovate the building, the county refused us the occupancy permit. It was a frustrating situation for me as the leader and for a young church. It knocked us down, limited our operations and raised some orange and red flags but courage picked us up. Courage is defined as strength in the face of pain or grief. Courage delivered strength to us when we needed it most. It opened the tap of joy for us to operate on. Courage helped us to soar again.

---

2 Corinthians 12:10 "Therefore I take pleasure in infirmities, in reproaches, in necessities, in persecutions, in distresses for Christ's sake: for when I am weak, then am I strong."

At the time of writing this book we have succeeded in completing and obtaining our occupancy permit for our two buildings totaling fifteen thousand square feet buildings in Montgomery County Maryland. To God be all the glory.

Psalms 31:24 "Be of good courage, And He shall strengthen your heart; All you who hope in the Lord."

There's one very important thing we need to notice about courage. You will never witness courage in someone who is at ease in Zion. Courage is seen in the person whose back is against the wall, when the odds are against them, when the pressure is on, when the flaming arrows are close, when the pain is intense, when the attack is at hand. Try courage. I am thrilled by the words of Winston Churchill, Britain's famous war time Prime Minister, who believed that *success is not final, as well as failure is not fatal: however, it is the courage to continue that counts.*

Do you feel that all is lost?

Do you think that it is the end of the road for you?

Do you think of a lifeline?

Embrace Courage*: 1Chronicles 19:13 "Be of good courage, and let us behave ourselves valiantly for our people, and for the cities of our God: and let the Lord do that which is good in his sight."*

Joab and his crew embraced courage to set into a winning battle against the Syrians. Brethren it takes courage to conquer.

Employ or Engage Courage: *2Chronicles 15:8 "And when Asa heard these words, and the prophecy of Oded the prophet, he took courage, and put away the abominable idols out of all the land of Judah and Benjamin, and out of the cities which he had taken from mount Ephraim, and renewed the altar of the Lord, that was before the porch of the Lord."*

Asa engaged courage in putting away the abominable gods in his nation. The employment of courage brought him and the nation back on track with God.

*Exercise Courag***e***: Acts 28:15 "And from thence, when the brethren heard of us, they came to meet us as far as Appii forum, and the three taverns: whom when Paul saw, he thanked God, and took courage."*

In all your pursuit in life, the exercise of courage is a boosting component for outstanding success in life. Paul exercised courage in order to be able to withstand all sorts of challenges and opposition targeting his mission.

Also Joshua wore the garment of courage and he made it to the promise land. Put on the garment of courage to operate in the realm of success.

Commitment:

Commitment keeps you on track in operating in the realm of success. The fact is, success is demanding; therefore commitment is a must to keep the tap of success flowing and thus minimizing the flaws. Pioneering an independent ministry in the state of Maryland after I've been in the state for a period of one and half year as an immigrant was demanding. I did majority of the manpower work, because the ministry was not equipped enough to afford to hire workers. Commitment was and is still the pilot that is ushering our ministry to its pivotal realm.

Commitment is not an option in the school of success but a mandatory subject

Commitment has great effect in your chase or drive for success. Commitment keeps your decisions in life intact. For instance, the couples make a decision to marry each other; however commitment is the key to help them to stay in the marriage. When you are committed to something or a project, you will eventually invest into that project. In that regard commitment will assure you of a positive outcome in the end. Commitment is not an option in the school of success but a mandatory subject or requirement that needs to be fulfilled before graduation. Commitment aligns you to your task. It generates the concept of faithfulness. In the New Testament dispensation we discovered the commitment and faithfulness of the Disciples of Christ. Majority of them were martyred for staying committed to the teachings of Christ. On the other hand Peter and Andrew were crucified but commitment kept them to the charge of fulfilling ministerial tasks.

Luke 19:13 "And he called his ten servants, and delivered them ten pounds, and said unto them, Occupy till I come."

Ruth stayed committed to Naomi, despite Naomi's request for her to stay in her native land of Moab.

Ruth 1:8 "And Naomi said unto her two daughters in law, Go, return each to her mother's house: the Lord deal kindly with you, as ye have dealt with the dead, and with me."

Ruth reaped the dividend of marrying to Boaz as a result of her commitment to Naomi. It was clear that Ruth path to success was attached to Naomi. Ruth discovered her assignment and she remained committed to the charge.

Ruth 1:16-18 "And Ruth said, Intreat me not to leave thee, or to return from following after thee: for whither thou goest, I will go; and where thou lodgest, I will lodge: thy people shall be my people, and thy God my God: Where thou diest, will I die, and there will I be buried: the Lord do so to me, and more also, if ought but death part thee and me. When she saw that she was steadfastly minded to go with her, then she left speaking unto her."

I am throwing a call for commitment with the end in mind. Put it on as a garment and you will not regret its effects. To commit to success is to yield and surrender oneself to the plans and purpose of God for your life. Do not allow any means of distraction to sway you away from God's purpose and plans for your life. Stay alert and follow the lead of God and you will make it.

Confidence:

Lack of confidence is detrimental to your pursuit of success. When confidence is absent individuals become easily intimidated. In the course of achieving success, confidence propels you to step out of insecurity with unwavering belief. Confidence is needed to conquer the challenges and disturbing walls on your path to success. Remember inferiority complex is a threat in building confidence. However confidence will help to establish and confirm your position and status in

> **To commit to success is to yield and surrender oneself to the plans and purpose of God for your life**

life. Confidence will also deliver unto you the rod of authority to operate with in life. Such authority will knock off the biggest enemy of confidence- inferiority complex. Jesus Christ is our perfect example of operating in confidence. He was confident to feed five thousand folks with just five loaves of bread and two fishes. His disciples were perplexed at the move. It took but confidence to deliver the expected result. Paul encourages us to be imitators of Christ.

Ephesians 5:1 "Therefore be imitators of God as dear children."

Let us imitate the confidence that Christ demonstrated during His earthly ministry. His confidence was second to none. He operated in power and authority over His contemporaries. Take into consideration that Christ in you is the hope of glory. You can operate in the same realm of confidence. Confidence is the conquerors tool for exploits. It was confidence that caused David to step up to the task for liberating his entire nation from the threat of the Philistines and their leader Goliath.

1Samuel 17:24-26 "And all the men of Israel, when they saw the man, fled from him and were dreadfully afraid. So the men of Israel said, "Have you seen this man who has come up? Surely he has come up to defy Israel; and it shall be that the man who kills him the king will enrich with great riches, will give him his daughter, and give his father's house exemption from taxes in Israel." Then David spoke to the men who stood by him, saying, "What shall be done for the man who kills this Philistine and takes away the reproach from Israel? For who is this uncircumcised Philistine, that he should defy the armies of the living God?"

Confidence eliminated the shame over hanging Israel at that time. David had confidence in God and himself and he won the battle with boldness.

My question for you today is: how confident are you? Brethren the concept of knowledge is the pillar for confidence. Confidence is anchored on what you know. Confidence is the principal remedy to defeat fear. Be reminded that the state of man operating in fear always lead to snare.

> **Confidence is the conquerors tool for exploits.**

For instance Daniel and the other three Hebrew boys –Shadrach, Meshach and Abednego became champions of faith based on the knowledge they had about God. Their confidence was high even in the midst of danger and catastrophe.

> *Daniel 3:16-17 "Shadrach, Meshach, and Abed-Nego answered and said to the king, "O Nebuchadnezzar, we have no need to answer you in this matter. If that is the case, our God whom we serve is able to deliver us from the burning fiery furnace, and He will deliver us from your hand, O king."*

They became candidates for exploits due to their knowledge of God. Knowing God is not the same as hearing about God. When you know God you are not scared of the oppositions;

> **Confidence is the principal remedy to defeat fear.**

Daniel 11:32 "but the people who know their God shall be strong, and carry out great exploits."

In my early years of ministry, demonic forces attacked me on several occasions but my knowledge of God has been my shield against such attacks. I remember being attacked by a cat in the night. We were sleeping in one of the rooms in our church back in Africa. The cat jumped one brother and came over to me to scratch and bite my toe. I woke up from my sleep and shouted the "blood of Jesus is against you". The cat screamed and jumped out of the window in haste, its speed caused the other brother to wake up in fear. This incident took place at around three O'clock in the morning. It was not a dream. Confidence in knowing God will cause you to be as bold as a lion.

Proverbs 28:1 "The wicked flee when no one pursues, but the righteous are bold as a lion."

It's amazing how bold you will become when you are full of confidence. Boldness is not intimidated by any situation. An individual anticipating success needs the full strength of boldness. A brother revealed to me a long time ago, how he was convinced and certain of a girl that he wanted to marry. The brother lacked the confidence to approach and disclose his intention to the girl. A few months later, the brother heard the minister publishing the bans of marriage between the same girl and another brother. The brother then realized that he had missed the opportunity of marrying somebody that he really loved and believed was destined for him. I actually spoke to the girl afterwards, she told me that she was also interested in the brother but since the brother did not disclose to her, she decided to move on. Imagine how lack of confidence robbed a man and placed inferiority complex on him. Regain your confidence, which will be your great strength of recompense.

Hebrews 4:16 "Let us therefore come boldly to the throne of grace that we may obtain mercy and find grace to help in time of need."

Confidence will give you the boldness and help that will be required of you in time of need. For instance, in the world of soccer a very good team will miss big chances and lose games as a result of lack of confidence. When the team lacks confidence most of the players will perform below par. Their full strength and capabilities become weak due to lack of confidence. In that regard I urge you to strive for confidence if success is your goal.

In addition, knowledge of God's word is another building block for confidence. The more of God's word you know the more confident and knowledgeable you become. In Christendom, the word of God is a powerful tool to engage with in our daily lives. The word of God is full of authority that will generate confidence and boldness to operate in any given situation. When the word is used appropriately, it is assured of delivering expected results. The word does not miss its target. The word is a potent force that will crush every obstacle that may stand on your way or path to success.

Hebrews 4:12 "For the word of God is quick, and powerful, and sharper than any two edged sword, piercing even to the dividing asunder of soul and spirit, and of the joints and marrow, and is a discerner of the thoughts and intents of the heart."

Spend time with the bible, which is one of the most effective avenues of knowing and learning the word of God. Read the word of God on a daily basis. If possible use a reading planner that will help you to read the entire bible in one year. Beyond reading the bible is to study the bible as well as meditate on the scriptures. Remember the more of God's word in you the more equipped you will become to confront any situation relating to your life.

Psalms 119:130 "The entrance of thy words giveth light; it giveth understanding unto the simple."

Light enters you when the word gains access into you. The word will also be a guide unto your path to success; it is imperative to know the word. Light eliminates darkness, extracts errors and gives insight and direction capable of leading to success. Light is a tool for correction and it is imperative to walk in the light and not in darkness.

Psalms 119:105 "Thy word is a lamp unto my feet, and a light unto my path."

God honors His word, so build a solid word foundation to gain confidence in life. Be determine to maintain the teachings of the word of God and by so doing success is guaranteed.

In conclusion, confidence is gained when you know your purpose. Acquiring comprehensive information about your assignment is a remedy for confidence in the school of success. Information will lead to formation. Seek knowledge and it will aid in all your undertakings. Before Nehemiah took the adventure of rebuilding the walls of Jerusalem, he made sure he gathered all the required information before he stepped out. No wonder he was full of confidence despite the oppositions of Sanballat the Horonite, and Tobiah the Ammonite.

> **Light is a tool for correction and it is imperative to walk in the light and not in darkness.**

Nehemiah 2:12-15 "And I arose in the night, I and some few men with me; neither told I any man what my God had put in my heart to do at Jerusalem: neither was there any beast with me, save the beast that I rode upon. And I went out by night by the gate of the valley, even before the dragon well, and to the dung port, and viewed the walls of Jerusalem, which were broken down, and the gates thereof were consumed with fire. Then I went on to the

*gate of the fountain, and to the king's pool: but there was
no place for the beast that was under me to pass. Then
went I up in the night by the brook, and viewed the wall,
and turned back, and entered by the gate of the valley,
and so returned."*

Nehemiah strived to know the situation of the broken walls as a prerequisite of his assignment. He was determined to understand and make the information acquired precisely clear and sorted out. It reminds me of the motto of my secondary school (Middle and High School), *'Knowledge is Light'*. Knowing your assignment is a key to success.

CHAPTER FOUR

Excel Beyond Limitations

We are living in a world that is full of limitations and barriers. Be reminded that you are destined to succeed. Limitations are set to limit your breakthrough and progressions in life. In this chapter you will discover prudent truth of breaking the limitations hindering your progressions in life. Understanding the limitations will inspire you to do something or take action.

Limitation: is basically a force that limits progression or achievement; it's a restricting factor. It sets boundaries that should not be overpassed. Limitations also place something or someone in a handicap condition.

In the current era, there are so many limiting agents that have deprived people with potentials from achieving their goals. Talents have been aborted due to limitations. Some of these limitations

> **Understanding the limitations will inspire you to do something or take action.**

can be mental or psychological, spiritual, or physical. As you continue to read this book, it is my prayer that God will enable you to break the shackles of limitations in your life. No matter the state of the limitation, be aware that God is able to bring an end to every challenging situation. My Bible reminds me *"God is able to do exceedingly and abundantly anything that we may think or ask for (Ephesians 3:20)."*

Limitations may tend to disable individuals, place a line of demarcation for people. Limitation can also keep you in one place; confine you to a certain level that you cannot go beyond. The answer is straightforward; there is nothing too hard for the Lord to do.

Jeremiah 32:27 "Behold, I am the Lord, the God of all flesh. Is there anything too hard for Me?"

You are born to succeed, and not to be a misfit. The original intent of God for you is to inherit the earth. Limitations cannot rob you of success. The name of Jesus is available for our use to break the borders of limitations. It is incredible to know and perceive the truth of the matter that there is no limitation that the power of the name of Jesus cannot conquer.

Excel: to excel is to do extremely well. It's also the concept of surpassing and outstanding in any given assignment. It's the state of overcoming obstacles, challenges, trials, difficulties etc.

Defer the Status Quo

Gideon a servant of God, was destined for greatness but limited to a status quo mentality. The force of limitation seized Gideon's breakthrough. The force of limitation will cause one to embrace and

> **You are born to succeed, and not to be a misfit.**

accept the status quo. I always remind the congregation to thank God for their present status but not to be limited to it. Life is designed to be progressive.

+ + ◆ ◆ + +

Proverbs 4:18 "But the path of the just is like the shining sun, that shines ever brighter unto the perfect day."

+ + ◆ ◆ + +

The trick of limitation is to make you complacent to the status quo. Sometimes the status quo may be comfortable, but I encourage you to see beyond it. Appreciate God for the present but see beyond that point. It's an underachievement. On the other hand some of the status quo is depleting and unacceptable. In addition, limitations will instill inferiority complex to condemn victims to accept and embrace such status. Status quo is a pathway for demolishing and dethroning any traits of progression.

Gideon nearly missed his breakthrough due to status quo mentality. When Israel needed help, the angel of the Lord confronted Gideon to rise up to the task to liberate his nation from the captivity of the enemies. (Look out for my book "From A Wimp to A Warrior"- A Biographical Study on the Life of Gideon) The statement and response of Gideon was defeating, he said, "my family is poor in Manasseh. "

Judges 6: 14-15 "Then the Lord turned to him and said, "Go in this might of yours, and you shall save Israel from the hand of the Midianites. Have I not sent you?" So he said to Him, "O my Lord, how can I save Israel? Indeed my clan is the weakest in Manasseh, and I am the least in my father's house."

The omniscient God knows everything, He knows that Gideon was a candidate for greatness and He picked on him. Wherever you are now is not the ultimate destination of your life. Gideon tried to ignore the call for greatness due to the notion of his family status. Matter of fact the Scripture states in *Ecclesiastes 7:8 "Better of is the beginning of things than the beginning thereof."* Break the grip of the status quo and force your way to success.

> **Appreciate God for the present but see beyond that point.**

Like Gideon, I was born and raised in Africa not to a wealthy family but to a family that struggled to provide basic provisions for daily living. At some stage in my life I was barricaded and caged in the trap of the status quo. Thanks to the redemptive effort of our Lord and Savior Jesus Christ that was made available for you and me. Since I accepted Christ I inherited the mindset of Christ that helped to break the inferiority complex that had entangled my mind for years as a result of the status quo. The apostle Paul in his letter to the Philippian church reminded us of this- *"Let this mind be in you, which was also in Christ Jesus, (Philippians 2:5)".*

The mind of Christ is the mind that does not embrace complacency but rather the mind of Christ is renewed every day. The mind of Christ is refreshed on a regular basis and strives towards fulfilling purposes in life.

Define your Godly Heritage:

Your heritage is clearly defined with the Lord. Defining your heritage will protect against the onslaught of limitations. As mentioned above, Gideon was constant because of the status in which he was. He did not recall that he was born with greatness. In most cases our upbringing may not reflect our Godly heritage or potentials. But be reminded that you are not an accident in this cosmos. God has a reason and purpose for your existence.

+ + ◆ ◆ ◆ + +

> *Judges 6:13 "Gideon said to Him, "O my lord, if the Lord is with us, why then has all this happened to us? And where are all His miracles, which our fathers told us about, saying, 'Did not the Lord bring us up from Egypt?' But now the Lord has forsaken us and delivered us into the hands of the Midianites."*

+ + ◆ ◆ ◆ + +

Being a minister of the gospel as well as a counselor, I have got the privilege to encourage a lot of people to break the grip of limitations in their lives by clearly defining their Godly heritage. Some have despised the family they were born into. Others have regrets over their nationalities. One of the concepts of this book is to rekindle the mindset of the reader about their godly heritage.

Galatians 1:15 But when it pleased God, who separated me from my mother's womb and called me through His grace..."

The apostle Paul clearly defined his godly heritage; he refused to be limited by no one. Despite all the humiliation and challenges that he encountered in life and in ministry, he was certain of his position in the Lord. He states "God separated me from my mother's womb...." He was aware of what was ahead of him. He was confident that he was destined for success.

Philippians 3:12-14 "Not that I have already attained, or am already perfected; but I press on, that I may lay hold of that for which Christ Jesus has also laid hold of me. Brethren, I do not count myself to have apprehended; but one thing I do, forgetting those things which are behind and reaching forward to those things which are ahead, I press toward the goal for the prize of the upward call of God in Christ Jesus."

I encourage you to emulate the apostle Paul; he refused to be intimidated; he ignores the inferiority complex and strives for the gold.

Being born and raised in Sierra Leone, there were so many challenges in my upbringing that I was faced with. For instance, the street and its environs where I lived did not have access to tap water. I had to walk over four miles to and fro to fetch water from another part of the city everyday doing three trips after school. I had to carry the container filled with water on my head covering the distance mentioned. Also before going to school in the morning, my daily assignment was to carry food for sale to the local market where my aunt was selling food (cookery). My regular assignments as the youngest boy in the house were too many and thus were hindering my time for studies and other school activities. There were times when inferiority complex used to shoot up in my life, causing some form of isolation and frustration in my life. Brethren I came to the realization after I encountered Christ that my Godly heritage has greater in store for me. Clearly defining your Godly heritage is a yardstick to defeat limitations. I realized that God has a purpose and assignment for me that no one else can fulfill other than me. What a turn around. My perception changed. My mind was renewed. I am walking in the victory of the Lord by clearly defining my Godly heritage and not drawing conclusions based on my national origin, family orientation or childhood challenges.

> *Psalms 126:1-2* *"When the Lord brought back the captivity of Zion, We were like those who dream. Then our mouth was filled with laughter, And our tongue with singing. Then they said among the nations, "The Lord has done great things for them."*

I encourage you in my writings of this book that "God will turn it around". No matter what the situation may be for you, God will turn it around.

Dream Big

Dreaming big is a platform to excel beyond limitations. Have a vision of the future. The notion of having a big dream will keep you on track in the race for success in life. Having a dream is a defining factor for an outstanding future. Dreams will help to keep your head up against any form of attack. When your dream is clearly defined it becomes a navigating tool that will dictate movements. Dr. Martin Luther King is a well-celebrated icon in the United States of America as a result of his dream. His dream of fighting against racism brought global recognition to him. His fight for equal rights and justice irrespective of complexion is paramount even in this modern era. In the Book of Genesis the Scripture described the dream of Joseph. He had a big dream, a dream that transformed nations.

Genesis 37:5-6 "And Joseph dreamed a dream, and he told it his brethren: and they hated him yet the more. And he said unto them, Hear, I pray you, this dream which I have dreamed."

Joseph's dream was too big. His dream provoked more strife and hatred from his siblings against him. Others do not easily embrace big dreams, but do not let the opinions of others limit the capacity of your dream. In the case of Joseph, his

The notion of having a big dream will keep you on track in the race for success in life.

own father and brothers were not convinced of his dream.

Genesis 37:9-10 "And he dreamed yet another dream, and told it his brethren, and said, Behold, I have dreamed a dream more; and, behold, the sun and the moon and the eleven stars made obeisance to me. And he told it to his father, and to his brethren: and his father rebuked him, and said unto him, what is this dream that thou hast dreamed? Shall I and thy mother and thy brethren indeed come to bow down ourselves to thee to the earth?"

As mentioned in previous chapters, Joseph's dream caused him a lot of commotions but in the end the contents of his dream was materialized. His brothers could not believe that Joseph was still alive. They thought the little boy Joseph was insignificant in their family so they tried to get rid of him, but Joseph did not get rid of his dream. Listen to Joseph's response to his brothers and siblings in return.

Genesis 50:19-21 "Joseph said to them, "Do not be afraid, for am I in the place of God? But as for you, you meant evil against me; but God meant it for good, in order to bring it about, as it is this day, to save many people alive. Now therefore, do not be afraid; I will provide for you and your little ones." And he comforted them and spoke kindly to them."

The fulfillment of your dream will bring your opponents to submission. Every aspects of Joseph's dream came to fruition. He was destined to succeed. I challenge you with the writing of this book not to be intimidated by the forces of dream killers. Their target is to kill your dream prematurely. In the New Testament Herod fought to get rid of Jesus in order to abort His dream of redemption for mankind. Identify dream killers and stay away from dream killers. Before I migrated to the United States of America in September of 2002, God showed me a clear vision in a hotel room in Abidjan. He gave me a vision to "Gather My People". Upon arrival in the United States I was zealous on embarking on fulfilling the vision. However I was faced with a lot of criticism and oppositions in a bid to discourage me from pursuing my dream. Despite all the oppositions from dream killers, God gave me the grace to ignore the dream killers and persisted to implement the contents of the dream. To God be the glory the vision was cast, and at the time of writing this book we have just completed the building of our first church auditorium. The building is ten thousand square feet in the heart of Silver Spring, Montgomery County Maryland.

In the school of success, dream, which can also be referred to as vision, is a paramount tool to success. Years back when I was in Africa I had a dream of preaching to a global congregation. In the natural world it seemed impossible because I was not even a pastor at that time. However I believed in the dream and continued with my service with the Lord. Least did I know that I would be broadcasting my teachings on television in mainland Europe as well as in the vicinities of the Washington DC Metropolitan area. Your dream will be very effective in the fight against limitations.

Diligence

Diligence is the mechanism for progression in life. Diligence is a vital component for fulfillment of dreams and purposes. The primary definition of diligence is 'hard work'. If you are aiming for success or to be at the top then diligence is one of the steps in the ladder that you will have to climb to get you to your desired goal. Success in life entails conscious acts of diligence. Diligence is the connecting rod to achieve greatness in life.

Proverbs 22:29 "Seest thou a man diligent in his business? He shall stand before kings; he shall not stand before mean men."

Diligence determines ones companion. It is believed that birds of the same feathers flock together. Diligence has the capabilities to change ones status for the best in life. **Purposes are accomplished by the employment of diligence.** Success in life is achieved by been diligent. It is very difficult for the lazy to acquire enviable success. Being lazy and idle is basically making an open invitation for poverty to take over.

Proverbs 10:4-5 "He becometh poor that dealeth with a slack hand: but the hand of the diligent maketh rich. He that gathereth in summer is a wise son: but he that sleepeth in harvest is a son that causeth shame."

Also the sluggard and lazy individual will find themselves in wants most of the time, while the diligent keep making progress in life.

Proverbs 6:9-11" How long wilt thou sleep, O sluggard? When wilt thou arise out of thy sleep? Yet a little sleep, a little slumber, a little folding of the hands to sleep: So shall thy poverty come as one that travelleth, and thy want as an armed man."

The smallest creature on the face of the planet- the ant is a professor in the school of diligence. The ant is a hard working creature that realizes that diligence is a necessary tool for success. Solomon referred to the ant as a perfect example for diligence. The diligent character of the ant enables it to prepare ahead of time.

Proverbs 6:6-8 "Go to the ant, you sluggard! Consider her ways and be wise, which, having no captain, overseer or ruler, provides her supplies in the summer, and gathers her food in the harvest.

Learn from the ant and make progress in your pursuit for success in life. Crush every form of complacency and idleness that may be holding and pulling you backward. Make effort to beat sluggishness on your path to breakthrough.

--- ✦ ✦ ✦ ✦ ---

Proverbs 12:11 "He that tilleth his land shall be satisfied with bread: but he that followeth vain persons is void of understanding."

--- ✦ ✦ ✦ ✦ ---

Drive Through

When you break the grip of limitations, you are on your way to drive through. Gideon drove through his homeland with dignity after he conquered his forces of limitations. After all the waiting and standing in the queue, it's important to take the next step. Ignoring the odds and pushing towards the goal is a propelling force to reach your destination. I'm fascinated by the drive through process of the Israelites leaving Egypt for the Promised Land. They encountered a lot of standstill but that did not deter them from driving through into their desired destination. Brethren, drive through to your Canaan land, you cannot drop in the middle of your journey. The Israelites would have dropped off from pursuing their goal when they faced the challenge of going through the Red Sea. However, their persistent mentality and determination saw them through to their Promised Land.

--- ✦ ✦ ✦ ✦ ---

Exodus 14: 15-16 "And the Lord said unto Moses, Wherefore criest thou unto me? speak unto the children of Israel, that they go forward: But lift thou up thy rod, and stretch out thine hand over the sea, and divide it: and the children of Israel shall go on dry ground through the midst of the sea.

--- ✦ ✦ ✦ ✦ ---

My experience in life and ministry has thought me to be persistent in reaching or striving towards achieving desired goals. The notion of going forward is a steering rod that helps to navigate individuals to not just give up but to pursue. The apostle Paul is strong on this note; his words to the church in Philippi is encouraging and worth considering for effective and efficient drive through concept.

> **When you break the grip of limitations, you are on your way to drive through.**

Philippians 3:13-14 "Brethren, I count not myself to have apprehended: but this one thing I do, forgetting those things which are behind, and reaching forth unto those things which are before, press toward the mark for the prize of the high calling of God in Christ Jesus.

Do not let yourself down, pursue your dream and go for it. More on follow your dream in chapter eight of this book.

> **The notion of going forward is a steering rod that helps to navigate individuals to not just give up but to pursue.**

CHAPTER FIVE

Delay is not Necessarily Denial

It is imperative to know that when things get delayed, it does not basically mean denial or failure. There are some successes that get delayed divinely. In order words the Lord is aware of the delay, God allows the delay to nurture and prepare individuals for uncontested breakthroughs and successes. The Lord makes everything beautiful in His own time. The time of God is perfect in all our undertakings. Humans tend to give up easily when things are not done at their own time. In spite of what we learned in the previous chapter on diligence and determinations, it is important to follow God's timing for your life. For instance it took several years for one of the most outstanding promises made to Abraham to be fulfilled. The promise of becoming the father of many nations was made when Abraham was seventy-five years old.

Genesis 12:1-4" Now the Lord had said unto Abram, Get thee out of thy country, and from thy kindred, and from thy father's house, unto a land that I will shew thee: And

I will make of thee a great nation, and I will bless thee, and make thy name great; and thou shalt be a blessing: And I will bless them that bless thee, and curse him that curseth thee: and in thee shall all families of the earth be blessed. So Abram departed, as the Lord had spoken unto him; and Lot went with him: and Abram was seventy and five years old when he departed out of Haran."

The promise did not come to fruition until when Abraham was one hundred years of age and his wife Sarah was also in her old age.

Genesis 21:5 *"And Abraham was an hundred years old, when his son Isaac was born unto him."*

In the midst of the delay, be aware of the fact that God is not slack concerning His promises.

Numbers 23:19 *"God is not a man, that he should lie; neither the son of man, that he should repent: hath he said, and shall he not do it? Or hath he spoken, and shall he not make it good?"*

The sovereign God is a keeper of His words, whatever he says he will do, that's exactly what he will do. He made a promise to Abraham that was delayed but eventually came to pass. If God said it, all you have to do is just to believe it. An Eighteenth Century American Educator

Amos Bronson Alcott once said that *Success is sweet and sweeter if long delayed and gotten through many struggles and defeats.* The success of Abraham did not come overnight. Abraham underwent a lot of challenges and battles en route to success. First he had to leave his kindred, the place of the known to the place of the unknown. Secondly he had to battle with his nephew a lot over possessions in the land. Third, Abraham tried to help God by following the wish of his wife to go to bed with her maidservant Hagar. Hagar eventually bore Abraham a son Ishmael that took the position of the firstborn son from Isaac the covenant child. Fourth, he had to endure the pain of letting go of Hagar and his firstborn son Ishmael out of the house at the dictate of his wife Sarah. However Isaac later inherited the covenant blessings of the firstborn son promised to his father Abraham. The apostle Peter dived into the character of the Lord and reminds the Church of Rome of God keeping to his promises.

> **The sovereign God is a keeper of His words, whatever he says he will do, that's exactly what he will do.**

2Peter 3:8-9 "But, beloved, be not ignorant of this one thing, that one day is with the Lord as a thousand years, and a thousand years as one day. The Lord is not slack concerning his promise, as some men count slackness."

In addition, some delays are divinely orchestrated. God permits the delay in order to prove a point. There are times that God will allow you to go through the valley of the shadow of pain and turmoil but the assurance is, God will never let you down. God can show up in your situation even when all the odds are against you. God is bigger than any predicament that may have overshadowed you.

Psalms 23:4 "Yea, though I walk through the valley of the shadow of death, I will fear no evil: for thou art with me; thy rod and thy staff they comfort me."

The valley of the shadow of death may come in diverse ways, such as obstacles and delays, sickness, fatal accident. In the midst of all those circumstances God is aware and is capable of turning the situation around. I encourage you not to be disheartened if you happen to be going through a drought or a delay. God will never leave you nor will He forsake you. It re-echoes the words God gave to Isaiah in chapter forty-three of the Book of Isaiah.

God permits the delay in order to prove a point.

Isaiah 43:2 "hence thou passest through the waters, I will be with thee; and through the rivers, they shall not overflow thee: when thou walkest through the fire, thou shalt not be burned; neither shall the flame kindle upon thee."

Some of the delays may be a test of character. Our reactions to delays and unforeseen situations define our character. Various patriarchs in the Bible passed the tests of their characters. You can pass yours too. The delay may turn out working for your good.

1Peter 1:7 "That the trial of your faith, being much more precious than of gold that perisheth, though it be tried with fire, might be found unto praise and honor and glory at the appearing of Jesus Christ."

Job on the other hand came out from his predicament as a winner despite suffering from terrible afflictions. The situation of Job was unbearable, but Job stayed with God, he linked with God throughout the test of his character and love for God.

> **Our reactions to delays and unforeseen situations define our character.**

Job 23:10 "But he knoweth the way that I take: when he hath tried me, I shall come forth as gold."

I can recall on countless occasions that I experienced delays and trials in my life and ministry. I have been through lots of pain, disappointments, discouragements and frustrations especially in my early years in ministry. There have been times when I thought it seems as if God is silent or distant from me. There are blessings that I am enjoying today that I thought I should have received years ago. Beloved, I can joyfully testify that God works in mysterious ways, He is never too early or never too late, He knows the time to deliver your results. It brings me to the notion that what God has destined for his children no one or nothing has the power to disannul what God has proposed. Sometimes things can get delayed and obstructed but they can never be snatched away.

Isaiah 14:27 "For the Lord of hosts hath purposed, and who shall disannul it? And his hand is stretched out, and who shall turn it back?"

Reading and meditating the miracle of Jesus raising Lazarus from death in John Chapter 11 helped me to identify four stages indicating that divine delay is not denial. Lazarus whose name means 'God help' was a very good friend of Jesus as described by John in his book. Lazarus siblings Mary and Martha were also supportive of Jesus' earthly ministry. The Apostle John mentioned about the love Jesus had for Lazarus and his sisters,

> **Sometimes things can get delayed and obstructed but they can never be snatched away.**

"Now Jesus loved Martha, and her sister, and Lazarus (John 11:5)."

It came to a time that Lazarus became sick. His sisters sent a massage to Jesus immediately of Lazarus condition expecting Jesus to make it on time to their house in order to prevent their brother Lazarus from dying. Jesus response to the request was very distinctive in assuring us that some delays are not denial but divine and also for the name of God to be glorified.

John 11:4 "When Jesus heard that, he said, this sickness is not unto death, but for the glory of God, that the Son of God might be glorified thereby."

Whatever delay you may be facing currently, see it as an opportunity for God to be glorified in your life. If that delay is from the devil in order to hinder your progress, I exercise spiritual authority over that delay now to be canceled completely in the name of Jesus Christ.

Disease Stage

It is at this stage when one begins to experience preliminary delay. At this point projects are getting infected by unforeseen forces and also things are not going as planned. Discouragement tends to creep in and make its way into your mind. When Lazarus felt sick, his sisters immediately dispatched the message to Jesus with a special caption that they taught could motivate Jesus to show up urgently.

John 11:2-3 "It was that Mary who anointed the Lord with fragrant oil and wiped His feet with her hair, whose brother Lazarus was sick. Therefore the sisters sent to Him, saying, "Lord, behold, he whom You love is sick."

Unfortunately Jesus did not show up. It seems as if Jesus was neglecting their call, but brethren it was not neglect but for God to prove a point. Jesus's delay to show up discouraged both Mary and Martha, they thought that time was against them and the chances for their brother's survival

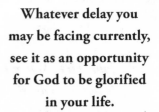

Whatever delay you may be facing currently, see it as an opportunity for God to be glorified in your life.

was getting slimmer and slimmer. The possibility of missing target dates begins to surface and looming around at this point.

John 11:6-7 "So, when He heard that he was sick, He stayed two more days in the place where He was. Then after this He said to the disciples, "Let us go to Judea again."

Have you been hit with stumbling block when you are targeting a particular date? What about the hindrances that has kept you from manifesting God's purpose for your life all these years? How many days, weeks, months or years are you behind from your target date? Jesus received the news about Lazarus sickness and stayed two more days before heading to Judea. I describe the action of Christ as purposeful delay. Purposeful delay is the concept or the circumstance that is used to unfold or to manifest God's glory over an impossible situation. Though Jesus loved Lazarus and his sisters, he purposefully delayed his coming into their house to prove the sufficiency of God's glory. If you have been hit with such calamities, I have good news for you. God can still turn it around. Do not allow doubt to come into your mind when things are getting delayed. The disease stage is the stage where you need to defy the threats of worries and lean on the sovereign Lord to turn things around in your favor. Strive to knock out any infectious traits that may hinder your progress as soon as you realize it. In the medical field it is adventurous and beneficial when diseases are diagnosed and treated from its preliminary stage. Take the situation to the Lord like Mary and Martha did, however eliminate the panic syndrome displayed by both Martha and Mary.

1Peter 5:7 "casting all your care upon Him, for He cares for you."

Death Stage

When something is dead, it literally means it stopped existing. In the context of this book, you will discover the omnipotent attribute of God on display. A songwriter wrote "for death could not hold him captive." The Lord Jesus has been consistent

> **Do not allow doubt to come into your mind when things are getting delayed.**

in defeating death and disease. Jesus responded to the call of Mary and Martha at the time when Lazarus was already dead. Martha exclaimed in despair and said Jesus if you were here our brother would not have died. They believed that Christ possessed the power to heal the sick, in order words; they were expecting Christ to tackle the Lazarus dilemma at the disease stage.

John 11:20-21 "Now Martha, as soon as she heard that Jesus was coming, went and met Him, but Mary was sitting in the house. Now Martha said to Jesus, "Lord, if You had been here, my brother would not have died."

However they were yet to experience the omnipotent power of God to raise the dead. Jesus responded to her with full confidence *"Your brother will rise again (John 11:23)."* Brethren if you have experienced or you are experiencing delay beyond the disease stage, be encouraged from the stance that Christ took. The Bible states Jesus Christ as the everlasting King, the same yesterday

> **In the context of this book, you will discover the omnipotent attribute of God on display.**

today and forever. Whatever He did in the past, he can still do in the present. May be your dream has hit a road block, your plans are at a standstill, no sight of progression anymore; be encouraged that the resurrection power of Jesus Christ can resurrect your dreams and visions again. When the due time came for God's intervention in Lazarus case, Christ spoke to his disciples to go over to Lazarus' house. He said to them *"Our friend Lazarus sleeps, but I go that I may wake him up."* His disciples were fully unaware of Christ statements of Lazarus sleeping. He openly told them Lazarus is dead.

John 11:12-15 "Then His disciples said, "Lord, if he sleeps he will get well." However, Jesus spoke of his death, but they thought that He was speaking about taking rest in sleep. Then Jesus said to them plainly, "Lazarus is dead. And I am glad for your sakes that I was not there, that you may believe. Nevertheless let us go to him."

Another instance is the case of Jairus' daughter. Jairus, a notable man in the society and one of the rulers of the synagogue faced with a deadly predicament; His daughter was seriously sick unto the point of death. Jairus came to Jesus and told him about his daughter's condition. Unlike the Lazarus situation Jesus decided to visit the house immediately upon receiving the requests from Jairus.

Mark 5:22-24 "And behold, one of the rulers of the synagogue came, Jairus by name. And when he saw Him, he fell at His feet and begged Him earnestly, saying, "My little daughter lies at the point of death. Come and lay Your hands on her, that she may be healed, and she will live." So Jesus went with him, and a great multitude followed Him and thronged Him."

———— ✦✦✦✦✦ ————

On their way to Jairus' house, someone came from Jairus' house with the sudden news of his daughter's death and thus suggesting the irrelevance of asking Jesus to visit the house since the daughter was already dead.

———— ✦✦✦✦✦ ————

Mark 5:35 "While He was still speaking, someone came from the ruler of the synagogue's house who said, "Your daughter is dead. Why trouble the Teacher any further?"

———— ✦✦✦✦✦ ————

When Jesus arrived at the house, everyone was mourning the death of the daughter, Jesus said to the people *"for she sleepeth."*

———— ✦✦✦✦✦ ————

Mark 5:38-39 "Then He came to the house of the ruler of the synagogue, and saw a tumult and those who wept and wailed loudly. When He came in, He said to them, "Why make this commotion and weep? The child is not dead, but sleeping."

———— ✦✦✦✦✦ ————

It is sometimes logical for one to loose heart or yield to the status when things are not going as planned or proposed. My goal is to inspire and challenge you to see beyond the tunnel of your present delay or predicaments, remember there is always a bright light beyond the tunnel.

It is at the death stage, where progress seems to be stalled, and it seems to be sleeping. Everything is going very slow like a snail movement. Jesus is capable of awaking your dream and to promote progress again and again. Christ woke up Jairus' daughter from her sleep; He will wake up your dream. He woke up Lazarus from his sleep; He will

remember there is always a bright light beyond the tunnel.

wake up your dream. The key factor to thrive beyond the death stage is absolute belief in God and your divine vision.

Mark 11:24 "Therefore I say to you, whatever things you ask when you pray, believe that you receive them, and you will have them."

Decayed Stage

Lazarus was already buried and was in the grave for four days. The Jews tradition believes in the notion that there are tendencies for the dead to rise again within three days of death. In case of Lazarus, he was dead four days before Jesus showed up in their house. It was clear evidence that Lazarus was gone for good.

John 11:39 "Jesus said, Take ye away the stone. Martha, the sister of him that was dead, saith unto him, Lord, by this time he stinketh: for he hath been dead four days."

At the decay stage, things are getting decomposed, negative rumors are perforating in the air about ones unwanted predicaments. These sometimes relate to our daily affairs, and the chances of succeeding are compounded by unforeseen circumstances that are beyond repairs. False rumors and allegations are spreading and circulating against you. Faultfinders and accusers are searching and waiting for an opportunity to criticize you due to the delay that may have compressed your pathway. It reminds me of the mockery of Hanna from her rivalry mate Penninah. Hanna experienced lateness in childbearing. Her mate used the decayed stage that surrounded her at that time as a catalyst for mockery. Are you faced with such dilemma? Be like Hanna, she refused to be intimidated by all the atrocities and rejections from within her household. She took a journey to Shiloh; and again Eli the priest misunderstood her. Hanna prayed relentlessly to overturn the predicament of delay that was in its prime stage of being decayed. In our communities most women have suffered from similar scenario that befell Hannah. For instance if a woman gets married and did not get pregnant after two to three years, that married woman will become a topic for discussion.

Prayer is the key component for overturning delay in the decayed stage. I will discuss a little bit on prayer in the next chapter. Jesus prayed over Lazarus and Lazarus came back to life. Brethren God can relieve you from the decayed stage; it's not over until God says it's over. God can change your smell with the fragrance of the Holy Spirit; His wind will blow on you again. It will eliminate every bad odor that may have surrounded your path to breakthrough. The woman with the issue of blood had all her possessions gone in a bid to cure herself from a stinking or decayed situation. This woman with the issue of blood was struck with calamity that isolated her from the community. However she received her breakthrough by ignoring all the odds that were against her and pressed towards the crowd to touch the garment of Jesus Christ.

Delivery Stage

At this stage, the reward will begin to show up in sequence. At the delivery stage goods are delivered and it is also at this stage that comfort is eminent. Jesus delivered Lazarus from the grave, despite being in the grave for four days. Christ exercised

Prayer is the key component for overturning delay in the decayed stage.

His omnipotent powers and delivered Lazarus beyond the odds and beliefs of the people. Mary and Martha, the sisters of Lazarus, were comforted at the resurrection of their brother despite the fact that they were expecting the intervention of the Lord earlier when Lazarus was at the disease stage.

John 11:43-44 "And when he thus had spoken, he cried with a loud voice, Lazarus, come forth. And he that was dead came forth, bound hand and foot with grave clothes: and his face was bound about with a napkin. Jesus saith unto them, loose him, and let him go."

This is a clear indication that God is able to do things that exceeds human concepts and imaginations. God operates in the realm of possibilities. God is credible and possesses potent attributes that will turn every situation around.

Matthew 19:26 "But Jesus beheld them, and said unto them, with men this is impossible; but with God all things are possible."

The delivery stage is the time of testimonies. At this stage the pleasure will erase the pain one has gone through in the other stages. Take into consideration, the joy of a mother delivering her baby after going through many predicaments during the pregnancy. My encouragement for my readers is to hang on and foresee the big picture. Basically have the end product in mind even at the raw material stage.

CHAPTER SIX

God has not forgotten you

It is easier to draw conclusions that God has forgotten us more especially when progress is slow. As we learnt in the previous Chapter 'Delay is not Denial', be assured of God's eyes on you. As the superintendent of your life, He watches over you diligently. He will never leave you nor forsake you, the infinite knowledge and providence of God means that He cannot forget you. The scripture states that the hairs on our head are numbered; literally meaning that God knows each and every one of us in depth.

Luke 12:6-7 "Are not five sparrows sold for two farthings, and not one of them is forgotten before God? But even the very hairs of your head are all numbered. Fear not therefore: ye are of more value than many sparrows."

The timing of God is always perfect; because He is an error free God. King Solomon was very well aware of Jehovah God being the magnificent timekeeper. The God who knows the season, He is not too late or too early. Situations and circumstances are beautified in his own time.

Ecclesiastes 3:11 "He hath made everything beautiful in his time: also he hath set the world in their heart, so that no man can find out the work that God maketh from the beginning to the end."

In striving towards success, the thought and awareness of God's timing for your life is very paramount. Majority of people have missed their timing, by rushing into things before its mature date and thus minimizing the strength of their full potential. Sensitivity to time is a key factor in the field of success. When things get delayed, it does not basically mean one has been forgotten. It is imperative for individuals to be sensitive to the time and understand the notion of divine delay.

> **The timing of God is always perfect; because He is an error free God.**

Ecclesiastes 3:1 "To everything there is a season, and a time to every purpose under the heaven."

Every purpose and vision has a maturity date. There are tendencies of encountering roadblocks when individuals fail to wait for the maturity date. Also the tendency of making mistakes is certain. Brethren don't be in haste, as this will interrupt the plans and purposes of God for your life. You have not been forgotten; it is just a matter of time for everything to emerge in your favor. God reserves the best for you-hallelujah.

In contrast, man may forget you. It is certain that man is liable to forget due to the notion that man is fallible. Understanding the term "forgotten" – it simply means to be left out; to be removed or not in one's mind; the concept of failing to remember. In contrast God cares for

> **Brethren don't be in haste, as this will interrupt the plans and purposes of God for your life.**

you so much to leave you out of His plan for the cosmos. God holds you in high esteem to fail to remember you. May I ask this question - have your loved ones forgotten you ever? Have you been in a state where you experience neglects from associates and loved ones? Well if you do, be encourage from this writings that mankind is fallible and has the tendency or capability to forget. Our Lord is the one that possesses the attributes of not forgetting or neglecting you.

Isaiah 49:13-16 "Sing, O heavens; and be joyful, O earth; and break forth into singing, O mountains: for the Lord hath comforted his people, and will have mercy upon his afflicted. But Zion said, The Lord hath forsaken me, and my Lord hath forgotten me. Can a woman forget her sucking child, that she should not have compassion on the son of her womb? Yea, they may forget, yet will I not

forget thee. Behold, I have graven thee upon the palms of
my hands; thy walls are continually before me."

<hr />

I have been forgotten on several occasions by loved ones and family, notably been forgotten unintentional by my aunt. This woman loved me so much however there was a time when she forgot completely about me. My aunt was dishing food and she completely forgot about me and failed to dish food for me. The dishes were so many that she forgot my own. To add to it, I was in the house when the incident took place. Just after she finished dishing the food she realized she has forgotten my own plate. She screamed- 'I have forgotten Abdul'. To summarize it all, she ended up giving me the pot to scrape the rest of the rice in it. I still did not know how you pronounce it in English but in Krio it is called (cra-wo'). The truth is I am a great fan of the so-called cra-wo' and I still crave for it to this day. Some of you may visualize the point that I am trying to make in this chapter. It was not all that pleasant in my early age because things were very tough for my family when I was in Africa. The major concern for most family then was to be able to provide a day's meal for the entire household.

As you are reading through this book, you are beginning to reflect on all those who have made promises to you and yet forget about you. The prophet Isaiah asks, *"Can a woman forget her suckling child? Yea they may forget"* The fact that a woman can forget her suckling baby shortly after all the turmoil that she may have gone through from conception of that child, to the incubating period of the child and to the pain of child delivery is an indication that nothing absolutely can surpass or exceed God's maternal strength for His creations. It is no mistake that man can forget you but there is one person who can never forget about you.

The person is the omniscience God. The prophet Isaiah makes it very clear that the sovereign Lord has graven you in the palm of His hands. Literally anytime God looks upon the palm of His hands your image will show up. You are right in front of his eyes, he is watching over you.

Isaiah 49:16 "I have graven thee upon the palms of my hands; thy walls are continually before me."

In the Old Testament of the Bible, there was an occasion when Joseph was in prison in Egypt alongside with the chief butler of Pharaoh. The chief butler had a dream while he was in prison, he did not have a clue about the meaning of the dream. A fellow prisoner Joseph interpreted his

It is no mistake that man can forget you but there is one person who can never forget about you.

dream. Joseph told the chief butler not to forget him when he is released from prison. Guess what, the chief butler forgot about Joseph.

Genesis 40:22-23 "But he hanged the chief baker: as Joseph had interpreted to them. Yet did not the chief butler remember Joseph, but forgot him."

My goal is to inspire and motivate you to make a positive change on how you articulate your position in the Lord. You are the apple of God's eye, there is no way He will forget you. God validates your success and breakthrough in life. When it was time for Joseph to emerge Pharaoh had dreams that he was desperately in need of someone to interpret his dreams. Pharaoh had exhausted every means to get his dream interpreted by magicians and astrologers. Unfortunately, none of the magicians and astrologers could interpret his dream.

Genesis 41:8" And it came to pass in the morning that his spirit was troubled; and he sent and called for all the magicians of Egypt, and all the wise men thereof: and Pharaoh told them his dream; but there was none that could interpret them unto Pharaoh."

It was at that time that the chief butler remembered about Joseph. People can remember you when they are in jeopardy not merely seeking your interest but for their own benefits.

Genesis 41:9 "Then spake the chief butler unto Pharaoh, saying, I do remember my faults this day."

The chief butler recalled of how Joseph interpreted his dream and the chief baker's dream. The thought only came when his master (Pharaoh) was already troubled because no one could interpret his dream. *Genesis 41: 11-12 "And we dreamed a dream in one night, I and he; we dreamed each man according to the interpretation of his dream.*

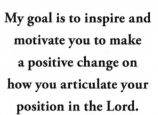

My goal is to inspire and motivate you to make a positive change on how you articulate your position in the Lord.

And there was there with us a young man, an Hebrew, servant to the captain of the guard; and we told him, and he interpreted to us our dreams; to each man according to his dream he did interpret.

However it was a pathway for Joseph to be released from prison and paved his way to fulfill destiny. When the fullness of God's time for your life comes, God can even use the most awkward situation to manifest His glory. It is my belief that God orchestrated the situation that no one was capable enough in Egypt at that time to interpret Pharaoh's dream so as to pave way for Joseph to be fulfilled.

Hebrew 6:9-11" For God is not unrighteous to forget your work and labor of love, which ye have shewed toward his name, in that ye have ministered to the saints, and do minister. And we desire that every one of you do shew the same diligence to the full assurance of hope unto the end."

The mother of Joseph, Rachel, also had delay in child bearing. She was the love of her husband Jacob. Her husband worked fourteen years for her father in order to be allowed to marry her. Her own father tricked her in favor of her elder sister Leah. The day for the consummation of her marriage, her father gave Leah to Jacob in place of Rachel.

When the fullness of God's time for your life comes, God can even use the most awkward situation to manifest His glory.

———— ✦ ✦ ✦ ✦ ✦ ————

Genesis 29:25 "And it came to pass, that in the morning, behold, it was Leah: and he said to Laban, What is this thou hast done unto me? Did not I serve with thee for Rachel? Wherefore then hast thou beguiled me?"

———— ✦ ✦ ✦ ✦ ✦ ————

Knowing the fact that Jacob was really in love with Rachel, he accepted to work for another seven years for Laban. Jacob was determined to marry Rachel at all cost to him, which he fulfilled.

———— ✦ ✦ ✦ ✦ ✦ ————

Genesis 29:27-28 "Fulfill her week, and we will give thee this also for the service which thou shalt serve with me yet seven other years. And Jacob did so, and fulfilled her week: and he gave him Rachel his daughter to wife also.

———— ✦ ✦ ✦ ✦ ✦ ————

Reflecting on all the mishap that took place in Rachel's life yet again she has to endure the humiliations and isolations from Leah and her children because she was barren at that time. It came to a time that Leah thought she will not be able to bear any more children for Jacob, she gave her maid to Jacob all in a bid to deprive Rachel. These are all the factors that added to her predicament of delays. However divine delays are not merely denials. The apostle Paul affirmed, "all things worked together for our good". Rachel ended up been the wife of Jacob that gave birth to the child who carries the prophetic purpose of God. She gave birth to Joseph a bit late, but the hand of God was on Joseph. It was rather unfortunate that Rachel died early and was not around to reap and enjoy the benefits of Joseph. The children of Leah eventually became partakers of the provisions that were generated from the child of a forgotten woman. Brethren it's never too late, God can still deliver your answer at the most appropriate time.

———— ✦ ✦ ◆ ✦ ◆ ✦ ✦ ————

Genesis 30: 22-23 "And God remembered Rachel, and God hearkened to her, and opened her womb. And she conceived, and bare a son; and said, God hath taken away my reproach."

———— ✦ ✦ ◆ ✦ ◆ ✦ ✦ ————

God did it for Rachel and her child became the savior of the family. Do not let doubt invade the territories of your heart when you are experiencing delay. The Lord is at work on your behalf to deliver the best to you. This is another scenario to learn from. It is not the quantity that really determines the magnitude of one's success but basically the quality of the product is what counts most.

———— ✦ ✦ ◆ ✦ ◆ ✦ ✦ ————

Genesis 30:24 "And she called his name Joseph; and said, The Lord shall add to me another son."

———— ✦ ✦ ◆ ✦ ◆ ✦ ✦ ————

It is my prayer for you that God will remember you for a great reward in the name of Jesus Christ. May you become a candidate to be remembered for long forgotten blessings by the time you complete reading this book.

> **Do not let doubt invade the territories of your heart when you are experiencing delay.**

In contrast some people have endangered themselves to have a second or third child and ended up having difficulties. Remember God knows you better and knows what is good and right for you. If He withhold from you, basically he is not denying you, he is preparing you for the best. Rachel lost her life in giving birth to her second child Benjamin. She wanted another child to compete in the rivalry between her and her sister Leah who was also her mate.

Genesis 35:18-19 "And it came to pass, as her soul was in departing, (for she died) that she called his name Benoni: but his father called him Benjamin. And Rachel died, and was buried in the way to Ephrath, which is Bethlehem.

I can recall a diligent woman I met with when I just arrived in the United State of America. She experienced delay in childbearing but she refused to give up on God. We prayed together and God answered our prayers and blessed her with a beautiful daughter. This woman stayed humble and content with her daughter the only child that she had and did not push for a second. I respect this woman; she is cherishing her daughter and praising God every day. I encourage you to remain firm in the Lord and appreciate whatever God blesses you with.

Mordecai also was remembered at the time when he and the Jews needed it most. Mordecai being a gatekeeper disclosed the plot to get rid of the king. The Scriptures say his deed was recorded in the Book of Chronicles.

Esther 2:21-22 "In those days, while Mordecai sat in the king's gate, two of the king's chamberlains, Bigthan and Teresh, of those which kept the door, were wroth, and sought to lay hands on the King Ahasuerus. And the thing was known to Mordecai, who told it unto Esther the queen; and Esther certified the king thereof in Mordecai's name."

Delayed blessings may sometimes come or granted when you are desperately in need for it. The life of Mordecai and entire Jews in the land were in jeopardy. Every Jew in the land was going to be slain after Haman forced his way onto the King and got the approval from the king who gave the decree to slay all the Jews.

Esther 3:6 "And he thought scorn to lay hands on Mordecai alone; for they had shewed him the people of Mordecai: wherefore Haman sought to destroy all the Jews that were throughout the whole Kingdom of Ahasuerus, even the people of Mordecai."

Just when Haman who was a catalyst of strife and hatred against Mordecai, thought he has gained ground over his so-called rival, God showed up in Mordecai's case. The King had a sleepless night because of Mordecai. Haman was disappointed at the final order. God will disappoint your enemies this time around.

Esther 6:1-3 "On that night could not the King sleep, and he commanded to bring the book of records of the chronicles; and they were read before the King. And it was found written, that Mordecai had told of Bigthan and Teresh, two of the King's chamberlains, the keepers of the door, who sought to lay hand on the king Ahasuerus. And the King said, what honor and dignity hath been done to Mordecai for this? Then said the King's servants that ministered unto him, there is nothing done for him."

I pray that God will be very active over your issues in the mighty name of Jesus Christ. I decree that whosoever that is holding on to blessings that are due to you will experience sleepless nights until they reward you with the blessings that are due unto you.

The following are my prescriptions to hang on to God in the midst of delay in order to overcome the roadblocks and setbacks that hinder success.

Trust: Basically Total Dependent on God is the Yardstick for Unstoppable Breakthroughs.

Trust in God

Isaiah 50:10 "Who is among you that feareth the Lord, that obeyeth the voice of his servant, that walketh in darkness, and hath no light? Let him trust in the name of the Lord, and stay upon his God."

Trust in His Word

Psalm 119:16 *"I will delight myself in thy statutes: I will not forget thy word."*

Trust in His Promises

2 Peter 3:9 *"The Lord is not slack concerning his promise, as some men count slackness; but is longsuffering to usward, not willing that any should perish, but that all should come to repentance."*

Truth: The Truth of God Precepts and Concepts is the Mechanism for Freedom and Liberty.

Psalms 119:93 *"I will never forget thy precepts: for with them thou hast quickened me."*

Proverbs 3:1 *"My son, forget not my law; but let thine heart keep my commandments."*

Tarry: Tarrying in Prayer is Necessary in the Building up to Success.

You can never go wrong by waiting diligently on the Lord. When things are delayed defeat the grip of delay by constantly tarrying in prayers. Prayer is basically given God permission to act on your behalf.

Tarry in Prayer

Hannah rejected the notion of being forgotten, she tarried in prayer.

1Samuel 1:11 "And she vowed a vow, and said, O Lord of hosts, if thou wilt indeed look on the affliction of thine handmaid, and remember me, and not forget thine handmaid, but wilt give unto thine handmaid a man child, then I will give him unto the Lord all the days of his life, and there shall no razor come upon his head."

Tarry in His Presence

The presence of God is the factory of joy.

Psalm 16:11 "Thou wilt shew me the path of life: in thy presence is fullness of joy; at thy right hand there are pleasures for evermore."

Tarry in Persecution

In spite of the persecution God still has you in mind.

> **Psalms 9:12 "When he maketh inquisition for blood, he remembereth them: he forgetteth not the cry of the humble."**

Tread: treading with God builds confidence when situations and circumstances are delayed.

Tread in His Path

Rachael treads on the path of God and God remembered her.

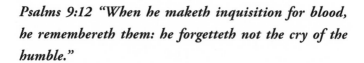

> **Genesis 30:22-24 "And God remembered Rachel, and God hearkened to her, and opened her womb. And she conceived, and bare a son; and said, God hath taken away my reproach: And she called his name Joseph; and said, The Lord shall add to me another son."**

In conclusion, **God is never too early or too late. God is always on target at the right time**. When God remembers his children and blesses them, He will make individuals forget about their shame.

Isaiah 54:4 "Fear not; for thou shalt not be ashamed: neither be thou confounded; for thou shalt not be put to shame: for thou shalt forget the shame of thy youth, and shalt not remember the reproach of thy widowhood any more.

May God replace everything that was designed to bring shame in your life.

CHAPTER SEVEN

Success Mentality

In this chapter, the goal is to develop your cognitive power and challenge your thinking faculty about success. The capacity of the mind has a big part in the pursuit of success in life. As stated in the previous chapters indicating the notion of success being your predestination; understanding the reality of how you are created in God's image and his likeness will support your thinking towards success. Realize the fact that it is the will and wish of God for you to succeed in life. It will be very vital to ignore the human and satanic success and think towards the covenant success. God wants us to strive towards embracing covenant success. Covenant success is divine and its God's desire for humanity. The Bible makes it clear that every good and perfect gift comes from above. So it is the wish of God for you to succeed and excel in life. This is how the mystery of God is unfolded through achieving success. The mystery of God is reflected on the thinking capabilities of mankind.

James 1:17-18 "Every good gift and every perfect gift is from above, and cometh down from the Father of lights, with whom is no variableness, neither shadow of turning. Of his own will begat he us with the word of truth, that we should be a kind of first fruits of his creatures."

Biologically a child's DNA matches that of the parents; as a born again child of God your DNA matches the reigning King of the universe who conquered defeat on your behalf by his stainless and sinless blood. Think right; if you have the blood of Jesus flowing through your veins you cannot be a failure

The capacity of the mind has a big part in the pursuit of success in life.

because the blood of Jesus is your symbol for success. No matter what you are going through at this moment, consider it as part of your resume. Yes it may be hard; it may be difficult, but think of the majesty of God, His magnificent attributes of success.

The Mind-set of Success

The mind of a man is a think tank. In a nutshell, man is a product of his thought. That is, what you think is what you become. "Phil 4:8"

You are the product of your thought. The scripture unfolds the syllabus of your life. It is my desire in this Chapter "Success Mentality" to inspire and motivate you to think soberly and eliminate all the negatives. If you can just come to the realization of the word of Paul to the church of Ephesus, you will grasp the power and ability of God beyond your own imagination. God has the ability and capability to do exceedingly and abundantly what we may ask or even think of.

"Ephesians 3:20 " Now unto him that is able to do exceeding abundantly above all that we ask or think, according to the power that worketh in us."

The ball is in your court; it is up to you to operate in the dimension of success by your thought process.

Proverbs 23:7 "For as he thinketh in his heart, so is he."

The Bible admonishes us to think of these things that are pure, strive to attain success and have a success mentality. Do not think negative or profess negativity. Let me tell you something, whatever you say is a product of your thinking. For out of the abundant of your heart the mouth speaks. If you think of succeeding in life you will succeed, but if you think of failure in life, you will fail. When you think of being a loser, then you will be a loser, but when you think of success, then success is yours.

"Success Mentality" to inspire and motivate you to think soberly and eliminate all the negatives.

Philippians 4:8 "Finally, brethren, whatsoever things are true, whatsoever things are honest, whatsoever things are

just, whatsoever things are pure, whatsoever things are lovely,
whatsoever things are of good report; if there be any virtue, and
if there be any praise, think on these things."

———————— ✦ ✦ ✦◆✦ ✦ ✦ ————————

I strived not to think of failure in whatever adventure that I will embark on. My determination is to think positive and crush every poverty mentality. Reflecting back to my early days in the United States of America, I was on course to achieve due to the fact that I refused to allow negativity to cripple my life despite the fact that things were not all pleasant. There was a brother I came in contact with who was also new in the country at that time. The brother had a poverty mentality or maybe greed mind-set. Whenever he goes to a store to buy something and they give him the price, he will then begin to calculate and compare prices back in Africa. He will not buy the thing but rather go without it as it seems expensive to him. This is what I call poverty mentality. One has to change your mindset, because when you talk about money, money is a currency, is a medium of exchange; and so you cannot expect to live Africa in America.

What is happening today, a lot of us that migrated from Africa to the United States of America are still living Africa in America. Our entire pattern and our way of doing things is the same African mentality regarding the cost of merchandize. How can you be residing in America, where they operate in dollar, but you want to buy things that are equivalent in Naira or in Leones or Franc? You must change your

> **My determination is to think positive and crush every poverty mentality.**

mind-set, you must change your way of thinking or else you will deprive and starve yourself of all the good stuffs. When you look upon yourself and conclude that you cannot purchase some stuff due to what it cost in a foreign currency, you are definitely making a big mistake. When you live in America and you have to live by the currency of your country of birth if you were not born in America, there is nothing wrong in living by that currency, but you have to live by the values of where you are. The scriptures state that *you will eat the fruit of the land*. You are bound to be a partaker of the fruit of the land where God has planted you.

Joshua 5:12 "And the manna ceased on the morrow after they had eaten of the old corn of the land; neither had the children of Israel manna anymore; but they did eat of the fruit of the land of Canaan that yea."

The children of Israel were partakers of the fruit of the land of Canaan. The Lord did not limit them just to the manna or the food of the Egyptians where they were in bondage for years.

If you think success then God can make you have outstanding success. When you think positively about yourself, you will eventually enjoy the fruits of your own positive thinking. I started thinking success over my life even when I was broke. The day God revealed and unveiled His plan and purpose for my life, I discovered from the words of the scriptures that I cannot be a failure. I immediately and intentionally began to walk towards that path. Before I migrated to America, one of my favorite songs then and even now is *"Colorful all is Bright I must get there."* I sang that song all the time. Don't call me to preach, because I will definitely sing that song, "Colorful all is Bright, I must get there." Despite the fact that I was sleeping on the benches in the church, but I knew my future was bright. Despite the fact that at that time I would use two suits to look like four or six, I still knew that my future is bright. I operated on that notion and I am reaping the products of where I set my mind-Hallelujah.

Mental Hygiene

Success mentality is anchored on the individual's mental hygiene. The mental hygiene has a big role in the pursuit of success as it also helps in pointing towards the outstanding product. Can I ask you a question today? How do you think of yourself? Paul says, *"Whatsoever things are true; think of these things"*. These are the things that should come into your mind. Don't think of failure when little things happen that do not favor you;, for instance, always dwelling on the time you were broke. Do not contaminate your mental hygiene with negative thinking. Change your mentality; you were not born to feed those negativities that crop up in your generation. The Bible says may this mind be in you that were in Christ Jesus. So think of success. If you want to succeed in life think of success. You are born to succeed but if your mind fails you then you are heading towards failure.

It takes your mind to conceive and convince you, that you are not a loser. Let it reverberate in your mind that you are not a loser. Having the mind-set of Christ as affirmed by Paul will cultivate success desires in you.

> **Success mentality is anchored on the individual's mental hygiene.**

Philippians 2:5 "Let this mind be in you, which was also in Christ Jesus."

Christ made it, Christ succeeded in fulfilling His mission on planet earth, and you will succeed because you are operating with a sound mind. Don't think of lack, failure or negativity on yourself. Think that you are what you think you are every day, every moment, and every second of your life.

> **Let it reverberate in your mind that you are not a loser.**

Develop a Success Mind-set

The society is polluted with heaps of negativities and negative reports. However it is up to you as an individual to succumb to the proliferation of the negative reports or defeat or reject such reports. In that regard may I ask you these questions: When you wake up in the morning what do you think of yourself? How do you think of your future? How do you think of the people around you? During the reign of Moses in the Old Testament dispensation, Moses sent twelve spies to go into the land to search, to observe, to bring a result about what is in that land. It was reported in the Bible, ten out of the twelve came with negative reports.

Numbers 13:32 "And they brought up an evil report of the land which they had searched unto the children of Israel, saying, The land, through which we have gone to search

it, is a land that eateth up the inhabitants thereof; and all
the people that we saw in it are men of a great stature."

———— ✦ ✦ ✦ ✦ ✦ ————

In Chapter Fourteen of the Book of Numbers, it is discovered that that the report of the ten spies caused weeping in the lives of the remaining Israelites? They made the people wept and cried with bitterness and sorrow. The negative report hindered their thoughts, strangled their trusts and also demolished their beliefs.

———— ✦ ✦ ✦ ✦ ✦ ————

Numbers 14:1-2 "And allthe congregation lifted up their
voice, and cried; and the people wept that night. And
all the children of Israel murmured against Moses and
against Aaron: and the whole congregation said unto
them, Would God that we had died in the land of Egypt!
or would God we had died in this wilderness!"

———— ✦ ✦ ✦ ✦ ✦ ————

It was only two of the twelve namely Caleb and Joshua who had the mind-set of success in spite of what they discovered in the land. Caleb and Joshua were outstanding due to their changed mentalities.

———— ✦ ✦ ✦ ✦ ✦ ————

Numbers 14:6-7 "And Joshua the son of Nun, and Caleb
the son of Jephunneh, which were of them that searched
the land, rent their clothes: And they spake unto all the
company of the children of Israel, saying, The land,

which we passed through to search it, is an exceeding good land."

There are tendencies that people may be operating on a programmed thought, but if those thoughts can be reprogramed positively, it will definitely yield positive results like we discovered in the life of Caleb and Joshua. For instance, I look at the meaning of the name Caleb in the Hebrew dictionary, it denotes Rabid, which means Dog, but Caleb was a man whose thought changed. Caleb was operating with a thought beyond the interpretation of his name. Caleb was not limited to negative thinking, he was thinking positively; he was one of the two men who came and stopped the people and interrupted them whilst they were giving Moses and Aaron the negative report. Caleb interrupted them and told them it is not what you think, yes we saw the giants, but I know for sure that we have a God who is well able, we have a God who is capable, and we have a God who is big enough to deliver positive outcomes for us.

Numbers 14:24 "But my servant Caleb, because he had another spirit with him, and hath followed me fully, him will I bring into the land where into he went; and his seed shall possess it."

Positive thinking will cause individuals to stand out in the midst of the cowards in the crowd. The Lord singled out Caleb and Joshua to possess the land as a result of their thinking mentality. It takes another spirit for you to operate in a mentality of success. Caleb was operating in another spirit. It is the spirit that sees beyond the present circumstances and norms. For one to operate in a success mentality one must see beyond their present positions. People who operate in success mentality are people who don't settle for the status quo. Success mentality will fight against negative reports and focus only to positive reports based on God's words and principles.

> we have a God who is capable, and we have a God who is big enough to deliver positive outcomes for us

---

Isaiah 53:1 "Who hath believed our report? and to whom is the arm of the Lord revealed?"

I am of the notion that one of the reasons why some people are caged into depravity is because of conceiving in their mind what other people are saying about them and their thoughts are cemented on those concepts. For example, some people are very quick in drawing negative conclusions;

> Positive thinking will cause individuals to stand out in the midst of the cowards in the crowd.

they will draw conclusions for a child without knowing what destiny holds for that child. No matter what others think about you, act upon the words of the Apostle Paul - *"Whatsoever things are of good report think of these things."* Don't think of failure because somebody tells you that you are a fool; in fact if you have an opportunity do not allow those negative words to build a nest in your mind. Paul says, *"Whatsoever things are pure, think of these things."* Think purely and positively in order to dream big. Change your mentality, change your mindset, and allow God to do the rest.

Remember as a man thinketh in his heart so is he. See yourself as a star and not a failure. See yourself as an Ambassador; don't see yourself as a loser. Refuse any form of intimidation because of the achievement of others. Protect the boarders

> **People who operate in success mentality are people who don't settle for the status quo.**

of your heart not to give any access to negative threats.

As you are reading this book, I urge you to get rid of negative thinking completely. Thoughts are expressed in words. The Bible describes an account of the woman with an issue of blood. This woman was possessed with the spirit of infirmity for twelve years. She was dripping with blood excessively to the point that she spent all her money in a bid to obtain cure from the disease. What delivered this woman was her success mind-set. The Bible said that she said to herself, when she heard that the crowd was coming by and Jesus was among the crowd and she said to herself, If only I can but touch the hem of his garment, I would be made whole. The woman with the issue of blood said to herself, I don't need to have a dialogue with him, if only I will have access. Her thought! If only I can have access to his garment, I don't need to touch his skin, just his garment, I will be made whole, said the woman with the issue of blood. She conceived it in her heart. She has that success mentality, and the Bible says when the crowd was so much, she pressed her way through because of her thought!! Thoughts are expressed in words and in deeds. She pressed her way, the crowd was stopping her but she moved and found her way; even though they were trying to prevent her from getting inside, she pushed her way because she had thought of something.

She touched the garment of Jesus and immediately she was healed from her infirmity.

Her thought delivered result for her; immediately she touched his garment she was made whole. May your thought deliver you the results you have been craving for all your life.

Thoughts are expressed in words and in deeds.

Discovery Mentality

In 1906, we had the first Airplane that flew up the air. This was contrary to human conclusions and definitions. In the year 1904 scientists concluded that it was impossible for metal to fly in the sky because of rust. But you know what happened? There were people who were operating in the dimension and realm of success. The success mind-set made the difference in getting the metal to fly and crushing the idea of impossibility.

There were these guys called the Wright brothers who operated in the realm of success. The Wright brothers took the challenge to counteract the conclusions of the impossibility for metal to fly as concluded by scientists in 1904. The Wright brothers got into discovery mode and activated their discovery mentality that is innate in every human being. Brethren the Wright brothers succeeded in their discoveries and in 1906 the first Airplane flew up in the air. The power of your thought! Engaging the mind to operate in the realm of discovery is fundamental to success in life. When

Invest in your thoughts and see how the image of success draws closer to you.

individuals enter into the notion of utilizing the full strength of their mental faculty, endless possibilities are imminent. Imagine the legacy established by the Wright brothers over a century ago. It is an extraordinary success that is traced to the discovery mentality. You can do it, activate your discovery mentality and begin to create success.

Isaac Newton is another legend in the school of discovery mentality. The three laws of mechanics discovered by Isaac Newton were gotten after eighteen months of school closure due to school strike and protest. Isaac Newton's father was a farmer. During the period of strike Newton engaged himself by working in his father's farm. It was reported that after the period of strike when school reopened, Newton had already transformed from a student to a professor because while his colleagues were thinking of negativity, Newton engaged his thoughts on how to make things happen. Invest in your thoughts and see how the image of success draws closer to you.

CHAPTER EIGHT

Follow your Dream

The concept of pursuing one's dream is paramount in achieving success. The dream may be the vision that God has unfolded for an individual to pursue. The scripture states, *"Where there is no vision the people perish."* In one of the chapters I mentioned about "Dream Big", however, one may have a dream or dream big but somehow reluctant or discouraged in pursuing that dream. One of the goals of writing this book is to motivate the readers to pursue their God's inspired dreams.

With strong passion and determination, one can follow one's dreams to the end. I am a living testimony of the benefits of following your dream. All through my journey to follow my dream, I tried to submit myself to God's sovereignty and His purpose for my life. I believe that God has given me creative gifts and talent. In order to activate and validate the creative ability of God in my

> **The concept of pursuing one's dream is paramount in achieving success.**

life, I asked myself these questions frequently - What moves me, what makes me uncomfortable? Once there is a desire to follow the dream, the dream can cause restlessness, actively engaging the mind, striving for mastery, walking circumspectly and so much more.

2 Timothy 1:6 "Wherefore I put thee in remembrance that thou stir up the gift of God, which is in thee by the putting on of my hands."

If there is a desire to follow your dream, then ask yourself the following questions. What wakes me up at night to pray and seek God's face? What makes me work so hard? Yes, for me it was building the house of God. A dream and passion that was huge in my mind. It was a dream or vision that God gave me in my hotel room in Abidjan, before my migration to the United States. The Lord gave me a vision and it reads, *"Gather My People."* With this in mind, I engaged myself with the spiritual disciplines of fasting and prayer seeking for God's directions.

Mathew 7:7 "Ask, and it shall be given you; seek, and ye shall find; knock, and it shall be opened unto you."

I remember reading through the pages of my Bible and discovered how David was passionate and determined to build a sanctuary for the Lord. Unfortunately, it was one of the desires of David that he was unable to accomplish. His son Solomon was the one who ended up building the temple for the Lord. I came to the realization that if God wants me to gather His people, He will definitely give me a place to put them. That is how I started a church building project.

In pursuit of the vision or dream of "gathering my people" we initiated the first service. The first place God took me was my adopted mother's basement with 17 people; then to a park hall where I can recall having leadership and board meetings inside the church van because we could not afford to pay for office space. The park hall was too small to accommodate both adults and children, therefore the Sunday school was under a tree in the park and when the weather got bad we used the church van that seated seventeen people to put both children and teachers. The engine had to be on of course to avoid little frozen fingers and shivering faces. It was not too long before we started the long waiting list of renting a Montgomery county public school space.

Think about a young black man from an impoverished country in Sierra Leone, West Africa, to come to America with nothing but a small suitcase and a dream - a dream to build a house for God. How farfetched. But one thing I know and believe is that if God gives a task, and one takes a step of faith to follow one's dreams, then the sky is the limit.

Alas! After the long wait to get into the public school cafeteria, I received an acceptance letter to go for the training to use the public school. It was a real dream comes true. Yes, a hall that takes over 400 people with classrooms and stage and parking spaces. Wow, what a wonderful accomplishment. With this I started seeing outwardly what God has placed inwardly - my own church that my flock can call home. That was

I came to the realization that if God wants me to gather His people, He will definitely give me a place to put them.

a drive to make a difference, a drive to stand out in the United States of America, the drive that shows how God moves. Oh what a drive it is when God is the driver.

I started looking for a place to lease; that did not go well because of rogues and thieves who thrive on innocent desperate pastors that need help. A group of so-called pastors and business people came in camouflage and reaped us of $10,000 in the hope of lending us money to renovate a site that we thought we could fix to make our own. After taking my money and wasting my time they disappeared into thin air. Then came other ideas to gather more money and get a land. The drive never stopped and the people never relented. The determination to build a church was so prominent that it was almost easy to get the people to give towards this dream, a dream to build God's house.

Yes after taking all the twist and turns and all the trainings that God wanted me to get, he brought me to a place that today I call *"City Of Light"*. It was not just a smooth ride or as easy as water passing under a bridge but rather it was a decisive choice to follow the dream.

When we got the site, the land was ready to be excavated, builders standing by, contractors signing contracts, members digging into their purses and bringing the money into the store house. And then came the hiccups, misfortunes, citations, permit delays, you name it. The question was when will the devil relax and let God's people reign. Indeed, God promised us a perfect finish on a rough road.

———— ✦ ✦ ✦ ✦ ✦ ————

Isaiah 45:2 "I will go before thee, and make the crooked places straight: I will break in pieces the gates of brass, and cut in sunder the bars of iron."

———— ✦ ✦ ✦ ✦ ✦ ————

But despite the entire setback, I still did not give up on my dream, a dream to build the house of God. One set back should not cancel your dream; in pursuit of your dream one set back should be considered as a roadblock that needs to be fixed. Brethren it would be amazing for you to know the location where we built City of Light Church, right in the heart of Montgomery County, one of the most profound areas that is very difficult to build a church. This is one reason why I am writing this book "You are Destined to Succeed." If God has destined you to succeed, He will make it happen anyway, anyhow and under any condition. Do not give up on your dream; keep it alive at all times. The dream should be made clear and precise. The prophet Habakkuk states in Chapter two of his book " *Habakkuk 2:2-3 "And the Lord answered me, and said, Write the vision, and make it plain upon tables, that he may run that readeth it. For the vision is yet for an appointed time, but at the end it shall speak, and not lie: though it tarry, wait for it; because it will surely come, it will not tarry."*

Keep following the dream, though it may tarry, delayed or encounter roadblocks. **The ultimate task is to get to the end and experience the fulfillment of the contents of your dream.** It's sometimes easy for someone to get distracted from his or her dream, sometimes get discouraged thinking that dream will never become a reality. Brethren just because the dream is still yet to reach it's climax doesn't mean the dream is aborted. Every dream has an appointed time for fulfilment so wait for it, follow it and it will surely come to pass.

CHAPTER NINE

Overcoming Challenges that come with Success

It is imperative to understand that success comes with challenges. To be successful is not just a smooth ride or as succulent as butter in bread, though you may enjoy the sweetness of it. There are tendencies or likelihood that there would be hiccups or challenges. This brings to mind the notion that obtaining success is one component but maintaining it is quite another vital key in remaining successful. In order to maintain success, one must be vigilant and strong to receive and combat the blows that come with it. I consider such arrows or persecutions that come with success as a test in sustaining the success achieved.

Consider yourself living a successful life. Your success will eventually provoke intimidations, blows and arrows from the devil and even from among your peers or contemporaries. Be reminded that Satan does not want to see God's children succeeding and thriving in life. Some of these blows may not be even farfetched; they may even come from close affiliates and acquaintances to intimidate you from enjoying your success. David became a victim of being humiliated by his own acquaintances primarily as a result of his achievements.

Psalm 55:10-12 "it is not an enemy that afflicted me, it's my own, my elect".

Operating in the realm of success takes courage, determination and dependence upon the strength of God. It takes the strength of God to overcome all the onslaughts from the enemy and its cohorts.

Psalm 46:1- "God is my refuge and strength, a very present help in trouble'.

God is your Refuge:

Success obtained from God should have God as the umbrella covering you in maintaining it. The refuge of God is a primary anchoring tool in overcoming challenges that come with success. Having God as the refuge will protect every achievement and of course, God is supreme

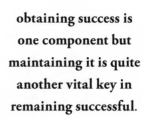

obtaining success is one component but maintaining it is quite another vital key in remaining successful.

and the devil knows it. Brethren, for as much as you have God as your refuge, do not be intimidated with the deceit and wrong statement and opposition that may come at you when begin to see the signs of success. God is big enough to cover his own from the attacks of the enemy.

Imagine the way the chicken protects its chicks by covering them with feathers. The chicken will take the blows for the chicks. Same scenario with God. He is able to take the blows for you if you make him your refuge.

God is your Refueling Fire

A full tank in a motor vehicle will run smoothly and cover mileages based on the capacity of the tank and mileage covered by the particular vehicle. With God being your refueling fire, your tank will never run dry. His words remind us in the scriptures that he has streams and rivers of water that we can always refuel from.

Brethren, for as much as you have God as your refuge, do not be intimidated with the deceit and wrong statement and opposition that may come at you

Psalm 46:4 *"Therefore, is a river, the streams whereof shall make glad the city of God, the holy place of the tabernacles of the most High"*.

Be assured that the challenges that come from man can be counteracted when one has God as his or her refueling fire. The strength of man is insignificant if God is not the fostering force behind the strength. David knows this and he emphatically makes it known that his strength is in the Lord. Nehemiah knows the importance of having God as his refueling fire.

Nehemiah 8:10 "The joy of the Lord is my strength".

Let God be your refueling fire and you will obtain strength to withstand the challenges that may come with success.

God is always ready to refuel us if we use the success that He gives us to feed and bless the people that are around us because the Bible says Kingdom wealth should be spread all around, he blesses you for his Kingdom sake. Anyone that is afraid to bless the people around them, in order to be in the mind of God for the refueling of his or her tank, will run dry. Brethren refrain from being reluctant to spread the success that the Lord has given to you. When you have gone up help someone to go up with you for this is what Kingdom success is all about. When God gives us riches, He gives us wisdom to maintain it and to multiply it. Therefore brethren we should not be afraid to share our success because God may not refuel us if our tank is half full or too full.

As we talk about refueling, think about the tank in your car and liken it to success in terms of material things. If you have more clothes in your closet than you have space for, your tank is too full. If you have more shoes than your closet can accommodate, my brethren, your tank is too full. How can God refuel a full tank? Therefore I urge you to share your success so that God will see the need to refuel your tank.

God is always ready to refuel us if we use the success that He gives us to feed and bless the people that are around us

God being my refueling fire is all I need to sustain the progress that I attained. In my work with the Lord, I found out that the challenges of life are most profound; hence the Lord encourages in: *Joshua 1:9"Have not I commanded thee? Be strong and of a good courage; be not afraid, neither be thou dismayed: for the Lord thy God is with thee whithersoever thou goest. "*

The scripture relates to the position of Joshua who succeeded Moses in taking the children of Israel into the Canaan Land. The Lord encourages Joshua to be strong and courageous in pursuing the task bestowed upon him. Joshua prevailed despite the battles and obstacles that he faced. Battles are real. As an individual I encounter battles most of the time. However my stance is to fight and keep fighting against the odds and stigma. In that regard, I anchor my faith and trust on the shoulder of the Lord. One of my favorite songs when faced with challenges is – "Through it all, I have Learned to Trust in Jesus, I Learned to Depend upon his Word."

> **God being my refueling fire is all I need to sustain the progress that I attained.**

God is your Reliever

In times of trouble and persecution God is your reliever. Depend on him and he will see you through. I have come to realize that success is not always blooming but also attracts envy and oppositions. When such things happen, look up to God as your reliever. *God is your present help in times of trouble....*

Psalm 46:1-3 "God is our refuge and strength, a very present help in trouble. Therefore will not we fear, though the earth be removed, and though the mountains be carried into the midst of the sea; Though the waters thereof roar and be troubled, though the mountains shake with the swelling thereof."

This Psalm gives hope and courage that one can become a conqueror as long as God is the ultimate source of help. Using God as your reliever, He will help in fighting against the enemies. God being your reliever is a great spiritual tool in overcoming discouragement, accusations, oppositions and manipulations in order to deprive you from enjoying the success attained. He is a present help in and out of trouble. He can be called upon at all times and His ears are always open to hear the plea of his children. Link up with Him and you will be able to overcome every challenge that may threaten the joy of your success.

I remember the oppositions I faced when I first got my real estate license as a Realtor in America. I entered into real estate market and made some sales that earned me some money. I received my commission without paying tax at that time. When I filed my tax at the end of the year, my CPA failed to itemize my expenses correctly, and it appeared as if I owed Internal Revenue Service and this can be stressful. But I was praying about the situation when the spirit of the Lord brought Psalm forty-six back to me that God is capable of delivering me

God being your reliever is a great spiritual tool in overcoming discouragement, accusations, oppositions and manipulations

out of that trouble. It gives me courage to know that even in times of despair and agony; you can be relieved if only you link up with your reliever - The Supreme God. God gave me direction to do a second opinion on the taxes. I spoke to my CPA again but he was very reluctant. He said he knew what he was doing and he would not change anything. And for sure he has a wealth of experience with a very good reputation. But I knew that it was a battle so I found another CPA who reviewed everything and refiled my taxes and I ended up owing nothing.

Psalm 46:5 "God is in the midst of her, she shall not be moved: God shall help her and that right early".

I got an early help as stated in the scriptures that relieved me from all my emotions and tensions. God made my eternal wars to cease. He made me prevail over the secret wars that I was fighting within myself.

Psalm 46:9 "He maketh wars to cease unto the end of the earth: he breaketh the bow, and cutteth the spear in sunder: "he burneth the chariot in the fire".

Brethren, be aware, or let me draw your attention to this very notion, that for as long as you are thriving and making progress, you are an instant target for the enemy because the devil considers your success as a defeat in his kingdom. Satan will always fight back in a form of challenge just to disturb your success. However, one thing for sure is the truth that Satan can only be barking at the wrong tree if only you rely on the supremacy of God's power. When God asked Lucifer what he was doing, he said he was roaming the earth, that is to say he was looking for whom to devour. God then asked him if he had tried his son Job, he replied that he cannot because God has put an edge around him. Satan knows those who have God's protection around them. Can God give Satan the mandate to test you today? You can only answer this question if you know for sure that God protects the success you have. He loves you enough to give you success and protects it.

James 1:2-3 "My brethren, count it all joy when ye fall into divers temptations; Knowing this, that the trying of your faith worketh patience.

Beloved let that resonate in you, as it will help you to triumph over the hurdles of temptation. Do not expect to get into the next level without trials. In the educational system, no teacher or professor will recommend a student for graduation without going through examination or tests. In addition, the exams or tests vary; the test questions for a middle school student are different from the test or exam that will be given

> **Satan can only be barking at the wrong tree if only you rely on the supremacy of God's power.**

to a high school or undergraduate student. The conclusion is that the magnitude of your test is an indication of the level you are about to attain. You are moving to the next level.

CHAPTER TEN

Handling Success

Consider this a reality that success is already achieved. In other words, you have moved from the dream stage to the reality stage. The reality is what needs to be maintained. To be right up there is glamorous but maintaining that glamour entails special effort. Brethren, be assured that success introduces you to the world because it comes with fame, prestige, status and the list goes on. On the other hand failure introduces the world to you. So whatever the world has to offer negatively, a failed life will most likely be on the receiving side of it. One may inherit success, but if not properly handled, it may slip out of your hands, which brings us to the cliché that *"millionaire die pauper"*.

The handling of success is very vital and should not be treated lightly. For instance, if there is a million dollar in one's account and one keeps deducting one dollar from that account every day, it will finish one day. Just as the contrary idiom goes that "a little drop of water makes a mighty ocean", likewise deducting from the account little by little without adding to it will eventually cause a drought. So it is with success;

having success without maintenance will lead to drought. Gaining and maintaining success are both vital in the field of success. For instance David worn the battle against Goliath and strived to maintain that status quo going forward.

Bless to be a Blessing:

It is my conviction that the first criterion in handling success is to be a blessing to others. The Book of Luke reminds me that the more we become a blessing to others the more our blessings increase.

----◆◆◆◆◆----

"Luke 6:38 "Give, and it shall be given unto you; good measure, pressed down, and shaken together, and running over, shall men give into your bosom. For with the same measure that ye mete withal it shall be measured to you again."

----◆◆◆◆◆----

The Lord promised us that he will give us wells that we did not dig and vineyards that we did not plant, and he said after we have eaten and are full we should not forget Him. This is success, and our God will not lie because he is not man neither will he change his mind because he is God. He is trying to tell us that when

> So it is with success; having success without maintenance will lead to drought. Gaining and maintaining success are both vital in the field of success.

success comes, there is a tendency for us to forget Him and even forget who we are in Christ. We should not let success negatively change or transform who we are; instead, success should amplify the good person that we are on the inside. If you are a giver, success should enable you to give more, if you are someone who likes to dress, wear name brand items, with success you should be able to bless other people. One thing I will say I admire about Oprah is that she gives gifts that she likes. If she likes Michael Kors bag, when she is giving gifts she will give Michael Kors bag to all those who cannot afford it.

As a Christian, we should be able to share our success with the people around us and if possible with the community and with the world as in the case of Oprah. The other side of the scripture that God encourages us in riches is when He said that after we have eaten and are full we should not forget the Lord our God who brought us out of Egypt. Here God is saying to us that success has the tendency to take us away from God. Believe it or not, the one thing that brings people faster to God is trials and tribulations. When we face trials and tribulations we are fast to make our room a place of worship, our shower a house of prayer, our children a congregation and our time a gift to God. So God is saying here, I am giving you a warning my son, after you have eaten and are full do not forget the Lord your God, do not forget to pray now that the storm is over, do not forget to fast now that the storm is over, do not forget to feed my people now that you have enough.

Sharing your success can come in different forms; for example, sharing your testimonies, becoming a father to the fatherless, helping the needy, supporting Kingdom work and things like that.

Border Protection:

It may seem as if you are fighting a war but truly it is a war to maintain what you got. If your success is not properly protected, it can be infiltrated by the opposition which in this case is failure. Protecting what you've already achieved or protecting your border is not just for the enemy but also for your own self. It is good to secure what you already have. Imagine all the defeats, all the battles you have conquered. Now get all your doors locked and windows closed in order to

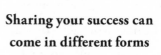

Sharing your success can come in different forms

secure what you have achieved. This is what I call border protection. Even the Bible reminds us that God protects and secures His own. He leads and guides His own against Satan and his cohorts and thus requires us to be protective of what we have attained. This is how we show that what He has given to us is valuable and precious. Your aid in that border protection is God as your commander in chief.

Psalm 91:1 "He that dwelleth in the secret place of the Most High shall abide under the shadow of the Almighty."

Anyone that hides under the wings of God is safe. His name alone is a strong tower and the righteous finds safety in it.

Planning ahead on how to retain success attained is pivotal in your border protection. Just as the saying goes, "failing to plan is planning to fail". I strongly believe that as a successful person, you strive to put the water fountain in place before you even feel thirsty to drink. In a nutshell, you should not be preoccupied and forget to

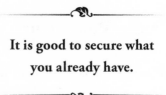

It is good to secure what you already have.

put the logistics in place for the drought. In the Old Testament, Joseph was a perfect example of a man who rose to supremacy because of his border protection concept. He interpreted the dream of Pharaoh and managed the principles and concepts of the dream for him. There was a seven years of plenty in which he used the border protection to put the fountain in place for the seven years of drought to come.

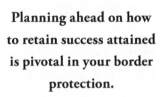

Planning ahead on how to retain success attained is pivotal in your border protection.

Genesis 41:34-40 "Let Pharaoh do this, and let him appoint officers over the land, and take up the fifth part of the land of Egypt in the seven plenteous years. And let them gather all the food of those good years that come, and lay up corn under the hand of Pharaoh, and let them keep food in the cities. And that food shall be for store to the land against the seven years of famine, which shall be in the land of Egypt; that the land perish not through the famine. And the thing was good in the eyes of Pharaoh, and in the eyes of all his servants. And Pharaoh said unto his servants, can we find such a one as this is, a man in whom the Spirit of God is? And Pharaoh said unto Joseph, Forasmuch as God hath shewed thee all this, there is none so discreet and wise as thou art: Thou shalt be over my house, and according unto thy word shall all my people be ruled: only in the throne will I be greater than thou."

Brethren, where you treasure, there will your heart be, so I urge you to maintain your treasure.

Broaden your Possessions.

As mentioned in this same chapter, bless to be a blessing. It is imperative that you broaden your possession. Yes it is good to share, but again, you have got to keep adding into the bucket before everything gets lost or dry. **Self-improvement is a pre-requisite here; you cannot just sit on what you have without aiming to improve on it.** This will help to prevent you from falling into the trap of complacency. Schedule some time for self-improvement on what you have attained. Look for new leads and jump into them cautiously.

Luke 12:16-18 "And he spake a parable unto them, saying, the ground of a certain rich man brought forth plentifully: And he thought within himself, saying, what shall I do, because I have no room where to bestow my fruits? And he said, this will I do: I will pull down my barns, and build greater; and there will I bestow all my fruits and my goods."

See nuggets below that will assist in broadening your possession

Act with courage towards new adventures

Courage to take the next step is pivotal in broadening your path.

Approach potential success gaining concepts diligently

Look and seek to break new grounds and diligently strive towards it.

Aspire to increase your success bank

The concept of increasing and expanding your success bank should be paramount.

Actively involve in expanding your terrain for success.

It's not enough to just aspire but to actively involve in expanding your territory is vital.

Glossary of Local Terms:

Cra-wo – Cooked rice crust.

Millionaire die pauper – Someone that was rich but died as a beggar.

ABOUT THE AUTHOR

Dr. Abdul K. Sesay is a highly anointed preacher, teacher, international speaker of the Word of God, whom God has raised to liberate his people from bondage through the inspirational teaching of the Good news of Jesus Christ. Dr. Abdul K. Sesay was born in Freetown, Sierra Leone, West Africa, to predominantly Muslim parents. Dr. Abdul grew up as a Muslim, attended Islamic elementary and high schools.

Dr. Abdul encountered the Lord in 1996. He attended the Freetown Bible School, Freetown, Sierra Leone and graduated in 1999. Prior to his graduation he received several leadership, evangelism, and teaching diplomas from various schools through both local and international correspondence training. After his graduation, he was called to help in the teaching Ministry of "Jesus Is Lord Ministry", in Freetown, Sierra Leone. After his conversion to Christianity, Dr. Abdul received a lot of rejection from his Muslim parents. He was always encouraged by the scripture in Psalm 27:10 "when my father and my mother forsake me, then the Lord will take me up".

In 1999, Dr. Abdul became a full time minister of the gospel serving as an associate pastor at "Jesus is Lord Ministry". God used him mightily, especially in the area of healing and deliverance.

Dr. Abdul moved to the United States of America in September of 2002 as a permanent resident. Prior to Dr. Abdul's move to the US, he had a vision and revelation from God, instructing him to bring together God's lost people – "Gather My People".

In March of 2003, in obedience to the vision and revelation God gave to him (Gather my people); Dr. Abdul co-started the "Kings & Priests Court International Ministries", with the Holy Ghost as the founder.

Dr. Abdul K Sesay graduated with the degrees of Master of Divinity and Doctor of Ministry from Liberty University. Dr. Sesay is currently pursuing a Doctor of Philosophy degree in Psychology (Mental Health and professional counseling). Dr. Abdul is serving as a pastor, teacher and prophet of the Word of God since the foundation of Kings & Priests Court Int'l Ministries Inc. to present. One of his major goals is to be a "father" to the fatherless, and this has given him a craving for helping and caring for orphans. Dr. Sesay is also the author of the award winning book –Remedies of Positive Living - *The ABC's of Living a Healthy and Positive Lifestyle.*

Dr. Abdul lives in Silver Spring, Maryland. He is blessed with two beautiful daughters, Abigail Absat Sesay and Anna Absatta Sesay.

OTHER BOOKS BY THIS AUTHOR

REMEDIES FOR POSITIVE LIVING-*The ABC's of Living a Healthy and Positive Lifestyle*

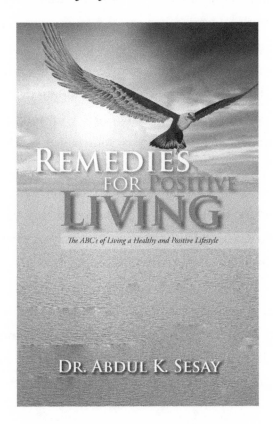

This book *REMEDIES FOR POSITIVE LIVING*- the ABC's of Living a Healthy and Positive Lifestyle will be a tool in your hand to keep you continuously joyful. It will give you all the juices and the ingredients to eliminate unpleasant circumstances and live a stress free life. A positive mood drives away any acts of failure and negativity in the life of every human being. As a patriotic citizen of heaven, positivity is your birthright. I personally believe that the following alphabetical sequence can effectively enhance your positive outlook.

FORTY- DAYS TURNAROUND

A Spiritual Warfare Tool in Pursuit for a Turnaround

Forty-Days Turnaround is a book on spiritual warfare. The book focuses on in depth spiritual warfare prayers and intercessions. The goal is to liberate your spiritual wellbeing in forty days period. Prayer is the focal point of the entire book. The concept of engaging in spiritual warfare is vital in our Christian community as well as for our daily living. Every day you wake up from sleep is warfare. Even when you go to sleep there are secret battles that are fought on your behalf by the ministering spirits assigned to your life. "Forty-Days Turnaround" will become a guiding tool to constantly stand in the gap in prayer for a turnaround. Also "Forty-Days Turnaround" will teach and help you to discover the power and strength in spiritual warfare prayers. Prayer is the key that is made available to everyone but it is the most neglected key that believers are refusing to take advantage of. Because prayer is one of the least activities of spiritual discipline among the average believer, it's my uttermost desire to deliver this book as a mechanism in the school of prayer that will enable you to take full advantage of the significance of prayer. Jesus, our perfect example for forty-day turnaround, displayed the value of forty-day preparation before he embarked on fulfilling his mission on earth. "Forty-Days Turnaround" is your weapon for everyday breakthrough. If you are looking for a turnaround in your business, marriage, hindrances, health and spiritual growth, "Forty-Days Turnaround" is the answer for you.

TWENTY-ONE DAY JOURNEY TO TRANSFORM YOUR PRAYER LIFE *Building a Legacy through Prayer*

This prayer journal will challenge you to embark on twenty-one days of prayer. The concept of twenty-one days, echo in my mind the experience of Daniel when he prayed for twenty-one days (Daniel 10:12-14).

Philosophers believe that anything that you do for twenty-one days will eventually become a habit. In this regard, I am encouraging you to build a solid prayer foundation within the next twenty-one days as you engage on this journey.

As believers, we need to have understanding in order to make an impact in life and in ministry. Without understanding, we will be out of order. Daniel set his face in prayer to receive understanding from God. The world is in need of answers to life threatening situations. As a believer you should desire to be the solution to the world's devastation.

CPSIA information can be obtained
at www.ICGtesting.com
Printed in the USA
BVHW031402020419
544382BV00001B/12/P